MADE IN AMERICA

T0310276

MADE IN AMERICA

*Self-Styled Success from Horatio Alger
to Oprah Winfrey*

Jeffrey Louis Decker

University of Minnesota Press
Minneapolis
London

Portions of Chapter 3 originally appeared as "Reconstructing Enterprise: Madam Walker, Black Womanhood, and the Transformation of the American Culture of Success." Reprinted from *The Seductions of Biography* edited by David Suchoff and Mary Rhiel. Copyright 1996. Used by permission of the publisher, Routledge: New York and London.

Portions of Chapter 5 originally appeared as "Gatsby's Pristine Dream: The Diminishment of the Self-Made Man in the Tribal Twenties," in *Novel: A Forum on Fiction* 28:1 (fall 1994). Copyright 1994. Reprinted by permission of the Novel Corporation.

Published by the University of Minnesota Press
111 Third Avenue South, Suite 290
Minneapolis, MN 55401-2520

Library of Congress Cataloging-in-Publication Data

Decker, Jeffrey Louis.
    Made in America : self-styled success from Horatio Alger to Oprah
    Winfrey / Jeffrey Louis Decker.
        p.   cm.
    Includes bibliographical references and index.
        ISBN 0-8166-3020-8 (hardcover : alk. paper). — ISBN 0-8166-3021-6
    (pbk. : alk. paper)
        1. Success—United States—History.   I. Title.
    BJ1611.D36   1997
    302'.14'0973—dc21   97-19568

Printed in the United States of America on acid-free paper

To Jenny

Contents

Contents

Acknowledgments

Although this book has many sources of inspiration, none is more important to me than the life stories of my grandmother and my mother. Both had circuitous, if not wholly atypical, routes to enterprising success for working women. I grew up hearing stories about my grandmother, Mary Marinaro, an Italian immigrant who, at fourteen years old, lied about her age to get a job as an operator with the telephone company. By the time I was born she had climbed the corporate ladder at AT&T into a midlevel executive position, which was as far as familial obligations and the corporate glass ceiling allowed. As I entered my teen years, a family crisis forced my mother, Cile Decker, into the paid labor force for the first time in fifteen years. She, like many women of her generation, turned to selling real estate. Beginning as an independent broker, she moved into management for a national real estate firm before starting her own company and making a success of it.

I began working on this project as a graduate student in American Studies at Brown University, where I became interested in exploring the literature of the self-made man and the history of the American dream. I owe a debt of gratitude to Brown's Department of American Civilization and to its Program in Modern Culture and Media for allowing me the intellectual space to explore a well-worn topic using nontraditional methods and materials. I thank my dissertation committee, Robert Scholes, Ellen Rooney, Neil Lazarus, and David Hirsch, as well as Mary Jo Buhle and George Monteiro, all of whom had the thankless task of supervising the initial stages of my discovery. During this period and after, Tricia Rose was a vital source of emotional support and intellectual camaraderie. George Lipsitz, who read various drafts of the project, never allowed his enthusiasm for my work to wane.

This book took its present shape during the 1992–93 academic year, when I was awarded an Andrew W. Mellon Faculty Fellowship in the Humanities at Harvard University. My thanks to the Mellon Program director, Richard Hunt, and the other Mellon Fellows for their advice and good humor. William McFeely, who presided over the group's activities, took every opportunity to encourage the book's development. Henry Louis Gates Jr. offered timely support in numerous ways, which included making available to me the resources of Harvard's Department of Afro-American Studies.

Over the past decade, my work on the book has benefited from the assistance of teachers, colleagues, and students at Brown, Wesleyan, and Harvard universities, Boston College, and UCLA. Individuals who read parts of the manuscript and/or discussed with me the general issues addressed therein include Nancy Armstrong, Houston Baker, Martha Banta, Randall Burkett, A'Lelia Bundles, King-Kok Cheung, Emory Elliott, Kevin Gaines, James Goodwin, Elaine Kim, Richard Ohmann, T. V. Reed, Janet Sarbanes, Richard Slotkin, Werner Sollors, Eric Sundquist, Leonard Tennenhouse, and Khachig Tölölyan. My editor at the University of Minnesota Press, Lisa Freeman, along with her assistant, Robin Moir, helped me through the trials of first-time authorship.

My family has been waiting patiently for this book to appear. I thank them for their support and unconditional love. My greatest debt is to Jenny Sharpe, soul mate and mother of our newborn, Maleka. Jenny, a champion talker, knows this book inside out. The sound of her voice, critical and caring, resonates through its every page.

As the archaeology of our thought easily shows, man is an invention of recent date. And one perhaps nearing its end.
—Michel Foucault, *The Order of Things* (1966)

Introduction

I locate this book within the long history of commentary that has transformed the self-made man into an archetypal myth and the ethos of entrepreneurial success into the quintessential American dream. At one time, the self-made man was vital to the national identity of the United States. Today, even as politicians campaign on the promise to rekindle the enterprising spirit that made the country great, pundits bemoan the loss of moral character—the very thing that self-making was supposed to cultivate in the individual. This book asks the question: What happened to the myth of the self-made man in America? If it is dead, what caused its demise? If it lives on, what form has it taken?

My study is indebted to two seminal books on rags-to-riches mythology: Irvin Wyllie's *Self-Made Man in America* (1954) and John Cawelti's *Apostles of the Self-Made Man* (1965).[1] Few studies since have attempted to revise the insights provided by Wyllie and Cawelti. The more discerning critics have remarked on what Garry Wills identifies as "the crisis of the self-made man" in our own time. In *Nixon Agonistes* (1970), Wills explains how, at the peak of social unrest during the sixties, the victorious presidential candidate embodied the old-fashioned morality of success in the eyes of an electoral bloc newly conceived as the Forgotten Americans. Ten years later, at height of the Me Decade, Christopher Lasch produced a jeremiad about the degeneracy of self-making in America. The author of *The Culture of Narcissism* (1978) lamented the fall of the Horatio Alger hero and his concomitant work ethic in a society seduced by consumerism's promise of instant gratification.

Made in America is, of course, no less influenced than previous studies by the era in which it was written. The wide range of enterprising individuals included in my study, as well as my interpretation of their narratives of self-making, are informed by the postmodern fragmentation of the singular subject of history. Thus, although this study is firmly situated within previous commentary that has transformed the self-made man into an archetypal figure of American literature, my objective is not to locate a single or univocal rags-to-riches story over the past century. Nor is it to simply celebrate new subjects of self-making, such as Booker T. Washington, Madam Walker, Mary Antin, or Younghill Kang. Instead, I am interested in the ways in which individuals engage narratives of success in complex and contradictory ways.

I use the word "narrative" rather than "myth" throughout my book in an effort to emphasize the self-made man as a rhetorical figure within U.S. national culture—an ideological sign that is neither timeless nor transcendent but historical and contested.[2] By placing mainstream narratives of individual uplift alongside less canonical ones, I examine how dominant culture shapes and is shaped by the cultures of subordinate groups. I read autobiographical and fictional expressions of class mobility as a contentious arena in which nontraditional entrepreneurs—working women, African Americans, and a wide range of immigrants—appropriate roles traditionally reserved for white, Anglo-Saxon men. I argue that the separation of gendered spheres, racial segregation, and nativism are constitutive of conventional stories of enterprise. While some marginal stories function primarily to legitimate middle-class formulas for uplift, others undermine the normative power of self-making.

This study also maps, over the past century, three shifts in the language of self-made success: from a nineteenth-century, producer-oriented emphasis on virtuous "character" to an early twentieth-century consumer-driven interest in psychological "personality" to a late-twentieth-century media-manufactured focus on the celebrity "image." During the early period of American industrialization, individual acquisitiveness was seen not simply as an end in itself but, ideally, as an expression of inner virtue. With the emergence of consumer culture at the end of the nineteenth century, a portentous transformation in narratives of self-making began to take shape. The alteration was marked by a shift from character to personality within the language of uplift. A consumer-oriented turn toward personality helped expand the terrain on which nonconventional entrepreneurs (women, blacks, immigrants) might imagine their lives according to the rags-to-riches formula. A greater inclusiveness coupled with the advent of personality diminished the moral authority of the traditional, white, Anglo-Saxon, male-centered narrative just prior to the Great Depression. With the emergence of the image-based celebrity alongside the post–World War II rise of corporate media culture, however, self-making made a return before century's end.

Part of my project is to interpret autobiographical statements on free enterprise symptomatically, for what the logic of personal uplift does not allow to be spoken. This means looking for the ghost in the machine, what Toni Morrison deftly identifies as the "active but unsummoned presences that can distort the workings of the machine and can also *make* it work."[3] Take, for example, President George Bush's controversial nomination of Clarence Thomas to the Supreme Court. When, at a 1991 Fourth of July holiday news conference, Bush introduced Thomas as "a model for all Americans,"[4] everyone knew what he meant. Later the same day, Senate minority leader Bob Dole put the appropriate media spin on the nomination by commending the nominee as "a man whose very life exemplifies the American dream."[5] He was right, of course, even if it might seem a bit startling that a black man who fulfilled the dream of success could serve as a representative American.

Yet there is a historical precedent to Thomas. Booker T. Washington, born into slavery, pulled himself up by his bootstraps and became the most powerful black leader during the Progressive Era (circa 1895–1915). Like his precursor, Thomas, the grandson of a sharecropper, rose from an impoverished background in segregated Pin Point, Georgia, to a position of political influence among conservatives in Washington, D.C. Long before Anita Hill's accusations of sexual harassment were made public, Thomas's handlers used what was referred to as the "Pin Point Strategy." Rather than highlight Thomas's credentials as a judge or his political views on abortion, the Bush administration maneuvered to sell their nominee to the American people as a black Horatio Alger hero.

The self-made black man was an image Clarence Thomas had himself fostered for years. Speaking as chairman of the Equal Employment Opportunity Commission for the Reagan administration, he wrote a letter to the *Wall Street Journal* defending "black self-help, as opposed to racial quotas and other race-conscious legal devices."[6] At a conference of black conservatives in the early 1980s, Thomas declared that only his grandfather's commonsense philosophy of hard work and self-reliance saved him from a life similar to that of his sister Emma Mae Martin, who was supporting four children on welfare. "She gets mad when the mailman is late with her welfare check. That's how dependent she is. What's worse is that now her kids feel entitled to the check, too. They have no motivation for doing better or getting out of that situation."[7] This statement, which Thomas later denied making, is as interesting for what it does not say as for what it does. Most notably, it fails to mention the circumstances—all too familiar to women living in poverty—under which Martin sought public assistance. While her brother was attending Yale Law School, Martin was abandoned by her husband and, as a result, worked two minimum-wage jobs to support her children. A family crisis ensued when an elderly aunt, who provided child care for the kids, suffered a stroke. Unable to afford day care for either her children or her aunt, Martin lived off welfare for four and a half years.[8]

The trajectory of Martin's life could not have diverged more widely from that of her brother. Nevertheless, on the eve of Thomas's nomination for the Supreme Court, she did not refute her brother's alleged show of disgust for her stint on welfare. Instead, in an interview with a journalist from the *Los Angeles Times*, she used the logic of self-making to describe her own plight: "You make your life for yourself. I had the opportunity to go to college if I wanted to, but I made the choice. I took care of the older people."[9] This autobiographical statement of failure equally depends on the language of individual uplift as do Thomas's reflections on his success. The power of self-help as a framework would explain why, during the initial Supreme Court confirmation hearings, Martin sat behind her brother, head bowed, in silent support. After Anita Hill's allegations were made public, when the stakes in the Thomas nomination shifted from black self-help to sexual harassment in the white-collar workplace, Martin receded into the background. She would remain completely absent from the media event that was the Thomas-Hill hearings.

The story of Clarence Thomas's sister Emma Mae Martin, even more than his own, draws attention to the normative power of the self-made man. I am less interested in the fact that she confessed her failure than the fact that she is obliged, by the agencies of power, to confess at all. The authority of confession, as Michel Foucault reminds us, is in the ear of the listener rather than in the voice of the speaker.[10] As such, normative power governs the forms for articulating knowledge. It also has the capacity to silence certain stories while finding a forum for others. In this case, the corporate media regulates "truth" by encouraging Martin to speak the language of self-made success.

The Rise of the Self-Made Man and the Triumph of U.S. Nationalism

Because the self-made man is a paradigmatic American figure, his study is useful for tracking historical changes to definitions of the U.S. nation, particularly in regard to race and immigration. Thomas's rise to the highest court in the land suggests the persistent lure of self-making as an expression of national identity. Historically, there has been a close fit between personal success and nation building. During the late eighteenth century, the nation was born from the American Revolution, while the self-made man was made possible by the fledgling concept of the modern individual. Up until the end of the eighteenth century, the word "individual" had a long-standing definition: it meant indivisible, "not cuttable, not divisible." According to Raymond Williams, the premodern individual was defined as "a single example of a group." Alternatively, the individual in modernity came to be considered as "a fundamental order of being."[11] Foucault's work elaborates on this development by showing that "man" is a recent invention that has its origins in the late eighteenth century. In an earlier period, it was assumed that God made men and that human beings should endeavor to understand the order of his world. The modern age inaugurates an epistemic shift whereby "man appears in his ambiguous position as an object of knowledge and as a subject that knows."[12]

Benjamin Franklin's late-eighteenth-century memoirs stage the ambiguous position of the enterprising man, who is not only an agent of history but also an object for meticulous study. The self-made statesman, while instructing his reader in "the bold and arduous Project of arriving at moral Perfection," appends to his list of virtues a daily chart for self-examination: "I made a little Book in which I allotted a Page for each of the Virtues. I rul'd each Page with red Ink so as to have seven Columns, one for each Day of the Week, marking each Column with a Letter for the Day. I cross'd these Columns with thirteen red Lines." In the spirit of the work ethic, he also reproduces a detailed outline representing an hour-by-hour breakdown of his daily scheme of order.[13] From Booker T. Washington to Lee Iacocca, aspiring self-made men have followed Franklin's example and deployed daily outlines, weekly routines, and monthly schedules as illustrations of the frugality and industry of their enterprising methods. As Foucault remarks in regard to the widespread deployment of timetables in modernity, "Precision and application are, with regularity, the fundamental virtues of disciplinary time."[14] Together, democracy and industrial capitalism demanded the transformation of the individual along the paradoxical lines of autonomy and freedom on the one hand, efficiency and atomization on the other.

The new meaning of the word "individual" gave root to the associated concept of "individualism," a word coined for popular use by Alexis de Tocqueville, author of *Democracy in America*. In the 1830s, while observing citizens of the new nation, he proclaimed: "*Individualism* is a novel expression, to which a novel idea has given birth." Tocqueville distinguishes the "democratic" idea of individualism, which suggests autonomy and independence, from selfishness, which "is a passionate and exaggerated love of self."[15] He also extends the new concept of individualism to the condition of the U.S. nation in the 1830s. Contrary to what one might expect, fifty years after the American Revolution, he found a surge in the demand for "independence" on the part of states rather than an increase in the federal government's power. Although "the Union offered, in several respects, the appearance of a single and undivided people," he insisted that, in the Jacksonian age, the "Constitution had not destroyed the individuality of the states."[16] Here, Tocqueville deployed the word "individuality" in its modern usage, meaning a unique entity.

The conflict between state sovereignty and federal authority on which the battle over slavery was waged resulted in the Civil War. It is a testament to Abraham Lincoln's vision that he was able to express, specifically in the Gettysburg Address, the importance of placing the nation's survival before states' rights. Marking the new sense of national unity, the noun "United States" would no longer be plural but singular.[17] This was the defining moment in the young nation's history, and historians have long described the outcome of the Civil War as the "triumph" of U.S. nationalism.[18] Although the birth of the U.S. nation dates back to the late eighteenth century,[19] American nationalism—the collective sense of Americanness and the institutionalized practices that promote such a feeling—is fully activated only in the second half of the nineteenth century.[20]

It was not until the late nineteenth century that nation-conscious traditions—such as ritualized observance of the Fourth of July and Thanksgiving, as well as flying Old Glory over all public schoolhouses—were widely institutionalized and disseminated throughout the country. The practice of patriotism was, as Wallace Evan Davies documents, "a sort of secular religion to unite the American republic."[21] Narratives of self-made success, too, were becoming increasingly accented by the language of nation rather than that of Christianity. Prior to the Civil War, writers such as Jacob Abbott composed popular children's fiction that both focused on solidly upper-middle-class heroes and taught boys and girls lessons in Christian piety. As John Cawelti points out, even when an antebellum author like Louisa M. Tuthill employed the newer concept of class mobility in her children's primer, the stories unequivocally preach the virtues of evangelical Protestantism.[22] At the dawn of the Progressive Era, however, even a good Christian such as Booker T. Washington could be heard lecturing his audience on nationalism: "The individual is the instrument, national virtue the end."[23]

In the twilight of the Progressive Era, Mary Antin, a first-generation Jewish immigrant and reformer, employed what she called "the American vocabulary" of the "self-made man" in an effort to crystallize, in the mind of her audience, "our national ideal of manhood."[24] Her statement explicitly weds the idea of the modern individual and the imagined community of the U.S. nation. Success literature was increasingly circulated to civic-minded activists throughout the late nineteenth and early twentieth centuries as a means of helping them instill middle-class values in the so-called dangerous classes.[25] The "new middle-class intelligentsia of nationalism had to invite the masses into history," explains historian Tom Nairn, "and the invitation-card had to be written in a language they understood."[26] Post–Civil War narratives of class mobility frequently stressed the enterprising hero's ability to demonstrate his connection to the national body.

For instance, at the opening of Horatio Alger's *Ragged Dick* (1868), the first and most-read "luck and pluck" fiction up through the Progressive Era, the bootblack hero asserts that his threadbare coat "once belonged" to the nation's founding father, General Washington. The orphan Ragged Dick is, by comic implication, cut from the same fabric as the father of the U.S. nation. The fact that the protagonist not only wraps himself in the flag but attempts to sell the clothes off his back to the same customer (at a "reasonable" price) suggests a link between a free country and the free market. When Dick's patron asks for change, the bootblack responds that he has not a cent: "All my money's invested in the Erie Railroad."[27] The transcontinental railroad, aside from being a powerful symbol of national unity, was the backbone of American industrialization and at the forefront of the transformation of the U.S. economy from competitive to corporate-monopoly capitalism.[28] Although Dick thinks of himself as a descendant of George Washington and a shareholder alongside Jay Gould, the same could not be said for those who built the railroads, mainly Irish and Chinese immigrants. Nativist attitudes are embedded in Alger's *Ragged Dick*, where the hero's antagonist, a juvenile delinquent named Mickey Maguire, is detected donning Dick's stolen Washington coat at the novel's end.[29]

With the official closing of the American frontier in 1891, enterprising men and the corporations they headed set their sights on expanding markets abroad. The imperialist impulse was found not just in industrialists and financiers, such as Edward H. Harriman and J. P. Morgan. In an era of monopoly capitalism and global colonialism, entrepreneurs of all stripes—including black nationalist leader Marcus Garvey and Edna Ferber's fictional saleswoman, Emma McChesney—scouted foreign markets for raw materials, cheap labor, and new consumers. In the popular *Emma McChesney & Co.* (1915), Ferber's protagonist targets trade with South American nations. Emma advocates expanding markets outside the United States because it "means a future and a fortune" for her New York–based company.[30] The expansionist inflection in Ferber's fiction was no doubt influenced by the country's awakened interest in new consumer outlets in South America prior to World War I. One observer, writing in 1911, noted that although the United States had recently "entered upon an era of commercial conquest" in the region, the North American nation had yet to live up to its manifest potential in regard to the Southern Hemisphere. He admonished his reader: "It is humiliating to an American to travel throughout . . . South America and see the trade which legitimately belongs to us slipping away to Europe." It inevitably led one to ask the questions: "What is the matter with the American business man? What is the matter with the American manufacturer?"[31]

Ferber answered critics of postfrontier American enterprise by targeting expanding consumer markets abroad. In an effort to beat the competition in her South American destinations, her military-minded heroine takes "just forty-eight hours to mobilize" from her base of operations in Manhattan. First, with her usual flair, Emma sells the idea of overseas expansion to her skeptical boss by implicitly appealing to national pride in the corporate race to claim the upper hand in global commerce: "If once I can introduce [our] petticoat and knickerbocker into sunny South America, they'll use those English and German petticoats for linoleum floor-coverings." On the eve of the invasion, the reader is informed that Emma "surveyed her territory, behind and before, as a general studies troops and countryside before going into battle." Next, she packs her weapons: sample trunks lined with skirts and knickers "calculated to dazzle Brazil and entrance Argentina." Finally, face to face with a corrupt Brazilian official, Emma coolly follows her New York training and offers him a bribe: "Her blue eyes gazed confidingly up into the Brazilian's snapping black ones, and as she withdrew her hand from the depths of her purse, there passed from her white fingers to his brown ones that which is the Esperanto of the nations, the universal language understood from Broadway to Brazil." As it turns out, the skirts are "self-sellers" in South America. After a four-month tour of duty, she returns home "gloriously triumphant," having conquered not only the alien customs of overseas businessmen but, more important, both foreign and domestic corporate competition south of the border.[32]

Having suggested that the historical possibility of the self-made man in America is underwritten by the late-eighteenth-century emergence of the modern individual and the spread of U.S. nationalism prior to the end of the nineteenth century, I want to examine two turn-of-the-twentieth-century developments that generate a crisis in the traditional narrative of success. The first is the shift from a producer- to a consumer-oriented society, which devalued the idea of moral character in the language of business achievement, and the second is the culture of personality, which allowed working women, African Americans, and nonnorthern European immigrants to appropriate stories of uplift and ultimately fracture the hegemonic discourse of class mobility.

From Character to Personality to Image

The Progressive Era marks a transformation in the United States from a producer- to a consumer-oriented economy. Although making money has always been an integral component of success in America, it began to undermine the art of virtue within the maturing consumer markets of the early twentieth century. At the turn of the century, the concept of personality was introduced into what had previously been an essentially character-based discourse of enterprise. As Warren Susman suggests, the word "personality" is tied to an emerging culture of consumption. He distinguishes between the new psychoanalytic idea of competitive personality and the older, quasi-religious concept of moral character, which evoked the spiritual calling that energized the self-starter in a producer-oriented economy.[33] My study develops Susman's speculative treatment of this transformation in a number of ways. I examine how the turn-of-the-century move from character to personality marked the democratization of narrative uplift. More specifically, I argue that the concept of moral character, which is coded as white, male, and middle-class, begins to recede within stories of self-making as women, blacks, and immigrants emerge as entrepreneurs. Toward the end of my book I also map a second historical transformation: from personality to image. This shift is, in large part, enabled by the proliferation of new electronic media after World War II that results in the simultaneous rise of the celebrity entrepreneur and effacement of character-based success stories.

The word "character" arises repeatedly in Franklin's eighteenth-century writing, the urtext of the modern self-made man. Franklin's utilitarian method of self-making was prefigured, in part, by the Puritan mission of bringing "works" into the covenant of "grace" through the Calvinist teaching that worldly success was a sign of God's predestined favor.[34] In his own attempts to practice "the Art of Virtue," Franklin aimed to cultivate "a perfect Character."[35] The concept of character that Franklin ascribes to the individual was of rather recent origin. Prior to the mid-seventeenth century, character was defined as a sharp instrument for making distinctive marks, engravings, brands, or stamps, and thus had no association with the human soul. Nonetheless, the idea of the individual deployed in Franklin's writing retained its older association with community (i.e., the individual as a single example of a group). For the purveyor of the traditional idea of character-based success, self-making and self-ishness were not synonymous.

The central importance that Franklin assigned to fostering the inner character of the yeoman farmer or fledgling entrepreneur was not lost on nineteenth-century purveyors of success. In his mid-century treatise *Elements of Success* (1848), Robert C. Cushman proclaimed that "the attributes of his character," rather than "the things which surround a man," were essential to personal achievement.[36] The concept of character foregrounded the spiritual salvation inherent in the Protestant work ethic in an effort to temper the avarice of enterprising men. As Irvin Wyllie discovered, "The doctrine of the secular calling provided the foundation for the religious defense of worldly success."[37] Many of the earliest advocates of self-help were clergymen who sermonized that man could serve God and Mammon simultaneously. Henry Ward Beecher, for example, lectured in 1844: "A good character, good habits, and iron industry, are impregnable to the assaults of all the ill luck that fools ever dreamed of."[38] Marketplace advancement, preached nineteenth-century apostles of the self-made man, was a sign of the cultivation of character. Onetime Unitarian minister Ralph Waldo Emerson's often repeated definition of the word—"Moral order through the medium of individual nature"[39]—is an attempt to resolve the conflict between God's sacred master plot and post-Enlightenment man's desire for autonomy.

Although after the turn of the twentieth century the word "character" no longer monopolized the discourse of enterprising success, it never abdicated its influence altogether. In 1900, soon-to-be president Theodore Roosevelt published an article on the American character and the idea of success. Roosevelt asserted that the "virile character" of "a thoroughly manly race" could be achieved not simply through amassing wealth but by means of "mental balance" and a "steadfast resolution"—"that assemblage of virtues . . . which we group together under the name of character."[40] Roosevelt, like many of his contemporaries, used the words "race" and "nation" interchangeably in an effort to draft the self-made man into the service of nation building.[41] Andrew Carnegie, a poor immigrant turned steel magnate and outspoken proponent of the American Way, reminded readers in *The Empire of Business* (1902) of his favorite theme: "honest poverty" as the "soil" on which "alone the virtues and all that is precious in human character grow."[42] His good friend Booker T. Washington extended the concept of character to his program for Negro education and enterprise. Despite criticism from black intellectuals that his ideas for uplift were outdated, the author of *Up From Slavery* (1901) championed "strength of character" to battle the temptations of consumer culture.[43] By maintaining the concept of character in consumer America, Roosevelt, Carnegie, and Washington activated what Raymond Williams calls the "residual" in dominant culture: an element of the past "still active in the cultural process, not only and often not at all as an element of the past, but as an effective element of the present."[44]

The twentieth century brought with it a transformation from character to personality, which was increasingly based on image making rather than inner calling.[45] The introduction of personality into the language of self-making no doubt energized the post–World War I spread of "New Thought" philosophy of success, which emphasized "states of mind rather than traits of character" by attempting to "codify in scientific form the 'laws' of personal magnetism."[46] Advertising executive and minister's son Bruce Barton told the story of Jesus Christ, the "founder of modern business," in his best-selling book *The Man Nobody Knows* (1925). What, asked Barton, was the quality that allowed the son of God to rise from poverty in a country village to become the greatest leader of all time? First and foremost, he possessed "the personal magnetism which begets loyalty and commands respect."[47] Before it became a best-selling book, *The Man Nobody Knows* was serialized in the *Woman's Home Companion*. Its original place of publication suggests that individuals other than white Protestant men were now targeted as consumers of success stories.

The modern fascination with personality helped expand the consumer market for narratives of the self-made man even while it undermined the narrative's traditional authority. Just as Progressive Era muckrakers were busy debunking the venerable character of the most powerful businessmen, individuals whose life experiences were marginal to mainstream stories of success began, at an unprecedented rate, fostering the winning personality. Ferber's representation of female enterprise offers a literary example. "Personality's one of the biggest factors in business to-day," announces an advertising executive in her 1914 novel *Personality Plus*. Although he explains that a young woman who gives off too much "charm" is incapable of controlling her personality in the world of sales,[48] the reader observes the heroine's personal magnetism as the source of her success in selling petticoats. "Her line is no better than ours," complains her competitor upon returning to the home office after being routed in South America. "It's her personality, not her petticoats."[49]

Traveling salesmanship was not the only profession in which marketing one's appearance was inseparable from selling one's product. The emerging business of cosmetics, pioneered by women such as Harriet Hubbard Ayer and Madam C. J. Walker, produced and was a product of the personality craze in America. "Cultivate the personality of the successful salesman," says Miss Fulton to Chungpa Han, the narrator of Younghill Kang's autobiographical novel, *East Goes West*. "Make yourself an attractive human being," she instructs, "for most of your customers will be women."[50] As Elizabeth Wilson reminds us, fashion is "essential to the world of modernity, the world of spectacle and mass-communication."[51] From Alger's poor boys, whose class mobility is usually marked by the acquisition of a new suit of clothes, to Madam Walker, who made millions styling hair, fashion frequently plays a conspicuous role in modern formulas for success. Or, as Emma McChesney puts it in regard to her prosperity in peddling petticoats: "I not only sell it, I wear it."[52]

In practical terms, enterprising women, immigrants, and minorities had greater access to the manufacture as well as the consumption of personality-enhancing products than, say, to steel or automobiles. The advent of personality within narratives of self-making was thus a two-way street. If consumer society allowed large numbers of nonconventional entrepreneurs to appropriate rags-to-riches stories for themselves, these individuals found an outlet for their ambition within expanding consumer markets.

Multicultural Narratives of Uplift
in Twentieth-Century America

Despite the fact that, after the Civil War, Abraham Lincoln was eulogized as the quintessential self-made man, the most publicized actors during the late nineteenth century were not politicians but a dynamic breed of entrepreneurs, such as Astor, Gould, Vanderbilt, Carnegie, and Rockefeller. By the turn of the century, however, opportunities for class mobility were in statistical decline due to the introduction of the corporate structure to business enterprise.[53] Paradoxically, the Progressive Era is also the moment when stories of self-made success were popularized, as never before, throughout American society. The paradox can be explained, in part, by understanding the extent to which the flourishing narratives of uplift helped bring marginalized individuals into the imagined community of the U.S. nation. Ironically, the popularization of the rags-to-riches formula caused an ethical crisis in traditional narratives of the self-made man prior to the Great Depression.

Beginning with Benjamin Franklin's memoirs, autobiography has been the authoritative mode within which to imagine the self-made man. However, recent studies of the genre demonstrate its complicity with the Enlightenment project of establishing the subject of history as white, male, and middle-class.[54] As such, autobiographies of enterprise composed by women and minorities are more likely to reveal the normative conventions of self-making. But what if, as in the case of most enterprising women and minorities, no formal autobiography exists? In an effort to locate nonconventional autobiographical expressions of class mobility, I have found it necessary to delimit the genre to include sources ranging from annual business convention transcripts to newspaper advertisements and television infomercials. In the absence of autobiographical statements, I locate stories of nonconventional enterprising individuals within either autobiographical writings of their contemporaries or popular fiction of the day.[55] My chapters read autobiographical and fictional expressions of class mobility as a contested arena in which nontraditional entrepreneurs (women, minorities, and immigrants) appropriate roles traditionally reserved for white, Anglo-Saxon men. Upon appropriating these popular models for middle-class uplift, they alter them. It is my contention that the expansion of the category of the self-made man to include working women, African Americans, and nonnorthern European immigrants contributed to the traditional figure's demise.

Chapter 1 examines autobiographical and fictional formulas for class mobility that, although inspired by enterprising opportunities in the Gilded Age, were widely disseminated after the turn of the century. I show how stories of entrepreneurial success confer "moral luck"—a secular version of divine grace—on their upwardly mobile protagonists while denying it to white ethnics and working-class heroes. Chapter 2 addresses the predicament of women who, during the Progressive Era, inhabited male-identified narratives of self-making. Not surprisingly, women's entrepreneurial agency was restrained by the imposition of the domestic ideal on their public activities. If popular literature generated imaginative models for female enterprise where none existed in reality, it nonetheless was marked by an ambivalence toward women's capacity to reconcile the tender qualities of femininity with the cutthroat world of marketplace competition.

Chapter 3 explores narratives of black enterprise by focusing on the political economy of racial segregation in America. What opportunities did Jim Crow have for realizing the dream of success? While the most prominent black leader of the day declared individual, merit-based uplift the standard by which to measure African American success, this focus distracted attention from the threat (imagined or genuine) that black-owned businesses posed to the market share of white entrepreneurs operating within the segregated economy. The threat of black enterprise became the primary, if rarely acknowledged, motive behind lynching. As a result, individualism—a term (as demonstrated earlier) central to traditional narratives of the self-made man—did not always take root in black America. Black enterprise was more likely to be an expression of racial uplift than personal achievement. Chapter 4 begins by examining the appeal of Marcus Garvey, a West Indian immigrant who implicitly addressed the problem of black individualism by envisioning a form of Negro enterprise that wedded personal uplift to a collective political campaign for African nationhood. This chapter also documents the changing climate of opinion toward "foreigners" during the Progressive Era and the Tribal Twenties. I evaluate the extent to which eastern European and east Asian immigrants both challenged consensus definitions of self-making and incorporated them into strategies for New World survival.

Chapter 5 examines the demise of the traditional self-made man in the 1920s. I read Fitzgerald's *Great Gatsby* not as the quintessential representation of the American dream but as its reverse: a canonical text that shows the self-made man in crisis. In order to recuperate his hero, Fitzgerald's narrator takes refuge in the nostalgic recovery of the American past underwritten by the logic of nativism. It was not until the 1930s that the term "American dream" was used. And, the concept was deployed not to celebrate but to critique, from the standpoint of the Great Depression, the moral bankruptcy of self-made industrialists since the Gilded Age.

Chapter 6 evaluates the ends of self-making within the context of postmodernity. The faceless structure of corporate America, consolidated after World War II, helped render the traditional enterprising individual invisible to the public eye. The expanding corporate media, however, found a new market for the self-made man: celebritydom. In one sense, selling the celebrity through magnetism takes the modern idea of personality to its logical conclusion. In another sense, media culture has not extended the idea of personality to the celebrity so much as effaced the old opposition between character and personality altogether. If, in the modern period, narratives of the self-made man *shifted* from a quasi-religious exploration of the inner soul (character) to a psychoanalytic examination of outward behavior (personality), image-based self-making *collapses* the distinction between inner self and outer appearance. As we move from an industrial to an information age, the figure of the self-made man is no longer principally the site of a utilitarian calling, behavior modification, or even economic production but, increasingly, of body image and consumer desire.

1

Class Mobility

Moral Luck and the Horatio Alger Formula: Andrew Carnegie

The fact that Horatio Alger's "luck and pluck" stories reach their peak in popular readership around 1910 has baffled literary historians. His cheap stories of boyhood achievement, although originally published in the second half of the nineteenth century, were reissued posthumously in paperback editions that sold more than one million copies annually by 1910. More copies sold each year between his death in 1899 until 1920 than they did in his entire lifetime.[1] Editorial abridgments of Alger's fiction turned what was, in his original work, a moral message with a monetary prize into tales of class mobility. Alger's portrait of poor boys, unlike the representation of working-class heroes in dime novels, does not remotely reflect the harsh economic realities of either the Gilded Age or the Progressive Era. Although his tales of virtue and good fortune recall an antebellum economic system of small manufacturers and agrarian farmers, it is inaccurate to conclude (as a recent commentator on success literature suggests) that "Alger is not a representative of his time, but a nostalgic spokesman of a dying order."[2] True, his protagonists are rarely industrial laborers; most have never even seen the inside of a factory. However, their ability to secure respectable white-collar work is characteristic of Progressive Era standards for middle-class success.

The turn-of-the-century production and circulation of rags-to-riches narratives needs to be understood as a symptom of the decline in opportunities for prospective entrepreneurs. Real-life prospects for upward mobility were, statistically speaking, curtailed once the corporate structure began to dominate the organization of American business. How, then, can we account for the fact that the literature of economic uplift—from Horatio Alger Jr.'s posthumous "luck and pluck" boy's fiction to self-improvement magazines such as *World's Work* and *Success*—reached the height of its popularity just prior to World War I? Despite the growing influence of the corporate way of life, many Americans would continue to valorize marketplace competition as a terrain of rugged individualism at least until the Great Depression.

Through principles I will term *moral luck* and *market pluck*, I argue that Alger's uplifting stories offered turn-of-the-century writers and their audience an outlet for reinforcing their belief in the residual concept of character-based success. Moral luck, I argue, is a secular form of grace that is coded as white, as masculine, and as middle-class. This chapter demonstrates how standard stories of class mobility confer moral luck on their heroes while denying it to industrial wage earners. For example, in *Ragged Dick*, Alger's most popular fiction, the honest hero labors without ever taking a step up the ladder of success. However, when he saves a wealthy man's drowning child at the book's end, Dick is handsomely rewarded with a new suit of clothes and white-collar employment. "Dick's great ambition to 'grow up 'spectable,'" Alger reassures his audience near the book's conclusion, "seemed likely to be accomplished."[3] Moral luck thus creates the context in which the display of market pluck is rewarded with a respectable occupation and income. As we will see, the language of moral luck is conspicuously absent from literature written by or directed to working-class Americans.

The primary innovation in the turn-of-the-century "luck and pluck" formula can be located in what is missing: didactic expressions of Christian morality common to self-help literature prior to the Civil War. Alger did not wholly abandon a Christian-based antebellum value system. As John Cawelti suggests, his stories are less tales of rags to riches than fables of rags to respectability: "Alger's formula is more accurately stated as middle-class respectability equals spiritual grace."[4] Market pluck, I would add, pays off only with luck guided by God's invisible hand. The author's promotion of the idea of respectable inner character allowed his audience to read a secular notion of class mobility into the imaginary landscape of virtuous success. For readers who lived through what historians call the nationwide "search for order,"[5] Alger's stories implicitly spoke to their fears about encroaching urbanization and addressed their anxieties about the fledgling reorganization of the workplace through corporate hierarchies.

The Gilded Age promise—that the opportunity to amass personal wealth was an American birthright—was threatened by turn-of-the-century economic upheavals and social dislocations. No self-made man of this era lectured more widely and wrote more prolifically on the twin topics of personal success and national progress than steel magnate Andrew Carnegie. Born in Dunfermline, Scotland, Carnegie emigrated to the United States in 1848 at the age of thirteen. His family lived in western Pennsylvania, where, a year later, he obtained a job as a messenger boy in a Pittsburgh telegraph office. Working for Pennsylvania Railroad in the 1850s, he rose from telegraph boy to steel master before the century was over. In between, he invested wisely in railroads and related industries, concentrated his resources in a revolutionary steelmaking process, acquired coal and iron-ore properties, and, finally, sold out to financiers who were putting together the U.S. Steel Corporation in the first decade of the new century.

Carnegie's favorite theme concerned building the moral character (honesty and integrity) of the enterprising man through market pluck (hard work and determination). He detailed the importance of pluck in his repeated discussions of the "advantages" of being "reared in the stimulating school of poverty."[6] Not surprisingly, when we turn to Carnegie's accounts of his personal uplift, the efficacy of strenuous market activity is sanctioned by the idea of moral luck. Up to this point, I have been borrowing loosely from philosopher Bernard Williams's theory of moral luck. In considering the importance of luck to moral life, he argues for a reassessment of the conventional (Kantian) notion that personal success is immune to luck and that the capacity for moral agency is available to any rational individual.

Instead, Williams demonstrates how the moral justification for one's acts is retrospectively constructed along the lines of constitutive luck.[7] Williams's notion of moral luck is useful for considering both autobiography, a literary genre defined by retrospection, and traditional narratives of the self-made man, where the excesses of rugged individualism are mastered by the art of virtue. Moral luck also manifests the turn-of-the-century crisis in character-based self-making, where the sacred notion of a moral life was threatened not just by the cutthroat requirements of marketplace competition but by new consumer temptations as well.

The language of moral luck is deployed in Carnegie's descriptions of his successful escape from his first job performing menial labor in a cotton factory. Employment of this type included long days, poor working conditions, and little pay. Despite the hardship, young Andrew imagines a better life: "But I was young and had my dreams, and something within always told me that this would not, could not, should not last—I should someday get into a better position."[8] Yet, rather than provide opportunities for entrepreneurial advancement, operating a boiler offers Carnegie a living nightmare. "I often awoke and found myself sitting up in bed through the night trying the steam-gauges."[9] The experience on the factory floor was so dark that he endured his work-related anxieties in complete isolation from his family.

Moral luck is bequeathed to Carnegie at the age of fourteen, when he found his salvation in the middle-class work environment of a respectable white-collar office. Here he is fortunate enough to receive what he calls his "deliverance" from the factory when he is offered employment as a messenger boy for a telegraph company in Pittsburgh. At this moment, Carnegie recollects in his *Autobiography*, "I got my first real start in life":

> From the dark cellar running a steam engine at two dollars a week, begrimed with coal dirt, without a trace of the elevating influences of life, I was lifted into paradise, yes, heaven, as it seemed to me, with newspapers, pens, pencils, and sunshine about me. . . . I felt that my foot was upon the ladder and that I was bound to climb. (38–39)

In an earlier autobiographical statement, Carnegie put it this way: "My 'Good Fairy' found me in a cellar firing a boiler and a little steam engine, and carried me into the bright and sunny office."[10] Carnegie's recollection of his transformation from dirty industrial laborer to immaculate office boy demonstrates the almost magical influence of secular luck on the narrative of the self-made man. Now settled into his white-collar occupation, he claims in yet another essay: "I entered a new world."[11] Carnegie models his early success on a character-driven narrative popularized in Alger's fiction. His boyhood desires echo no one so much as Ragged Dick, who wistfully states to his friend: "I'd like to be a office boy, and learn business, and grow up 'spectable."[12]

Moral luck is not distributed equally among the poor boys of Alger's fiction. In *Ragged Dick*, the reader is presented with a stereotypical Irish bully named Mickey Maguire, whose fall into delinquency is mirrored by Dick's ascent toward grace. Good fortune is never bestowed upon Mickey because, whereas Dick's ambition is always virtuous, his Irish rival's is not. Mickey, we learn, has been in prison "two or three times for stealing."[13] Even when, as in a later Alger story titled *Mark, the Matchboy* (1869), Mickey returns and is reformed, his rise to the top is cut short. "In capacity and education," judges Alger's narrator, "he is far inferior to his old associate, Richard Hunter [formerly Ragged Dick], who is destined to rise much higher than at present."[14] As Cawelti reminds us, "the old maxim 'No Irish Need Apply' still held for Alger."[15]

The tendency to leave "whiteness," as a racial category, unmarked in our reading of standard narratives of upward mobility has contributed to its transparency and normative power. Yet, in Alger's juvenile stories, new immigrants are far less likely to receive the divinity of moral luck. In his *Autobiography*, young Andrew Carnegie must shed his ethnic identity before he enters the order of the self-made man. Like Alger's antagonist, Carnegie was a recent arrival to the United States. For the thirteen-year-old Scotsman, assimilation was a prerequisite for acquiring the moral luck that would elevate him into the "new world" of American middle-class respectability. The reader of Carnegie's *Autobiography* learns that, just prior to being blessed with good fortune, he was transformed from working-class foreigner to middle-class citizen. In order to gain employment as a messenger boy in a telegraph office, he is compelled to reject his Scottish identity by literally and symbolically disassociating himself from his father. Arriving at the office for his interview, young Andrew, not wanting to look foolish in front of his father, asks him to wait outside. Carnegie recalls: "I insisted upon going alone."

> I was led to this, perhaps, because I had by that time begun to consider myself something of an American. At first boys used to call me "Scotchie! Scotchie!" and I answered, "Yes, I'm Scotch and I am proud of the name." But in speech and in address the broad Scotch had been worn off to a slight extent, and I imagined that I could make a smarter showing if alone with Mr. Brooks than if my good old Scotch father were present, perhaps to smile at my airs. (37–38)

Carnegie sheds his immigrant identity by imagining himself as an isolated individual, distanced from the Old World community he associates with his father. A symbolic orphan, he swallows his foreign accent and dons attire "usually kept sacred for Sabbath day" (38). He is now prepared to receive the divinity of moral luck.

Hard Luck: John McLuckie

When working-class characters make an appearance within a conventional rags-to-riches story, they draw attention not only to the limits of class mobility for industrial laborers but also to the discourse of nativism that sometimes licensed their bad luck. It was the Mickey Maguires of the world, rather than the Richard Hunters, who were more likely to labor in the factories. One such working-class individual was "Honest" John McLuckie, who emerges in the middle of Carnegie's *Autobiography*, and whose name seems to mock the moral luck required for class mobility. McLuckie was a key actor on the stage of the famous 1892 Homestead strike, which, as labor historians argue, undermined the ideals of labor republicanism and helped make corporate capitalism triumphant.[16] Homestead was the largest and most modernized open-hearth steel mill of its day. Prior to Carnegie's purchase of the plant in 1883, its workforce was organized into a half-dozen unionized labor lodges of the Amalgamated Association of Iron and Steel Workers. Ironically, it was the power of the union and a history of labor unrest at the plant that enabled Carnegie to purchase the mill below market price from its previous owners. The details of the Homestead strike are well documented. On management's side, Carnegie's trusted associate, Henry Clay Frick, handled the contract negotiations and the strike itself. Frick, who was fiercely antiunion, produced an inflexible contract proposal that was intended to force a strike and ultimately break the union. Despite efforts by the Amalgamated Association to keep contract negotiations open, on the last day of June 1892 all 3,800 union and nonunion Homestead employees walked out.

The strike was immediately supported by the town of Homestead, led by its mayor, John McLuckie, who was a skilled worker at the mill. Three hundred Pinkerton guards were brought in by Frick on July 6 in order to protect the company's property and its replacement workers. Violence erupted and lasted for twelve hours; by the end of the day, four Pinkerton guards were dead and many more were injured. The Homestead plant, however, was untouched and it remained under the control of the strikers for four days. On July 10, the governor of Pennsylvania ordered in eight thousand troops to restore Homestead to its owners. Within a week the plant was operating with replacement labor.

Andrew Carnegie was conspicuously absent from strike negotiations and, at the time, uncharacteristically silent about the events surrounding it.[17] His *Autobiography*, composed approximately fifteen years after the strike, is interesting for what it both expresses and refuses to say about Homestead.[18] Carnegie inserts a pair of documents from uncorroborated sources into a twelve-page chapter titled "The Homestead Strike," where the author explains his opposition to hiring replacement workers while absolving himself of responsibility for doing just that at Homestead. The two documents were supposedly authored by laboring men: one is a letter from the strikers at Homestead appealing to Carnegie for paternal guidance; the other contains McLuckie's words of kindness for his former boss fifteen years after the strike. These documents function to confirm the virtuous character of Andrew Carnegie, venerated self-made man. However, they also point to the limits of moral luck, within a story of class mobility, for an "honest" laborer such as John McLuckie.

The first document is a telegram that Carnegie claims to have received belatedly "from the officers of the union of our workmen" once the strike was already under way and out of the steel magnate's hands. It reads: "Kind master, tell us what you wish us to do and we shall do it for you" (232). According to Carnegie's biographer, Joseph Frazier Wall, the author knew at the time he was composing his autobiography that the document did not exist: "nowhere in his personal papers could [Carnegie] find such a telegram."[19] In 1912, Carnegie employed a top executive to track down the cable or, if unlocatable, to obtain confessions from former Homestead employees to having signed the telegram. The executive's efforts proved unsuccessful on both counts. Nevertheless, Carnegie published the cable in the Homestead chapter of his book in an apparent effort to boost his reputation as a champion for the rights of the workingman.

The second document concerns the whereabouts of John McLuckie after the Homestead strike and the personal testimony regarding his former boss, Andrew Carnegie. It is important to remember that the leaders of the strike, McLuckie included, were blacklisted from working in steel mills in the United States ever again. Moreover, within a decade after Carnegie Steel defeated the Amalgamated Association at Homestead, unions in the steel plants were essentially defunct and were not able to organize effectively in such industries until the Great Depression. The author's portrait of McLuckie is a secondhand account provided by John C. Van Dyke, who posthumously edited Carnegie's *Autobiography*. Van Dyke reports that he accidentally discovered McLuckie working as an unskilled laborer in a Mexican mine in 1900. McLuckie was "careful not to blame Mr. Carnegie, saying to me several times that if 'Andy' had been there [at Homestead] the trouble would never have arisen." Upon being informed of Van Dyke's discovery, Carnegie claims to have sent Van Dyke the following telegram: "Give McLuckie all the money he wants, but don't mention my name." Following these instructions, Van Dyke informs McLuckie of his incredible good fortune without disclosing its source. To Van Dyke's surprise, McLuckie declines the generous gift: "He said he would fight it out and make his own way, which was the right-enough American spirit. I could not help but admire it in him" (235–37).

Within Carnegie's narrative of self-made success, even an exiled working-class hero can display a work ethic attributable to the American Way. However, he cannot accept the benefits of middle-class morality. Later, Carnegie provides a postscript to McLuckie's hard-luck story. He claims that, within the year, Van Dyke happens upon McLuckie once again, now gainfully employed by a railway company in Mexico. So that McLuckie "might not think unjustly of those who had been compelled to fight him," Van Dyke discloses the source of his prior offer of financial assistance. "McLuckie was fairly stunned, and all he could say was: 'Well, that was damned white of Andy, wasn't it?'" (237). For Carnegie, the reluctant robber baron, his act of charity and McLuckie's response vindicated his personal responsibility at Homestead and his treatment of labor in general: "it indicated I had been kind to one of our workmen" (238). Carnegie, it was said, never tired of hearing the story of his ex-employee's final disclosure.

I would suggest that Carnegie's identity as a self-made man obliged him to interpret McLuckie's use of the word "white" as meaning fair, generous, and decent. Is this how McLuckie meant it? We will never know for sure, but we would be well advised to situate the statement within the context in which it was spoken. The former mayor of Homestead was, as one biographer points out, "the most unbridled spokesman of the rebellious strikers."[20] Even Carnegie acknowledges that, after Homestead, McLuckie lost everything: employment, money, family, and country (236). It thus seems more likely that the exiled burgomaster used the word "white" sarcastically, as in the sentence: "That was very white of you!" With this in mind, McLuckie's declaration constitutes a thinly veiled denunciation of his former boss. By conjuring the ghosts of Homestead past, McLuckie's momentary presence in Carnegie's *Autobiography* has the capacity to rupture a narrative of moral luck.

The Limits of Luck: James J. Davis

In Horatio Alger's self-improvement literature, upward mobility is bestowed on those poor boys who embrace a white-collar corporate identity. As Daniel Rodgers flatly states, whatever else success writing might be, "it was not a literature aimed at the industrial wage earner."[21] Alternatively, the working-class dime novel was a site for imagining and interpreting life in and around the factory. Michael Denning demonstrates how these stories measured success by standards sometimes foreign to the middle-class morality of Alger's "luck and pluck" formula. For instance, while dime novelist Frederick Whittaker penned cheap stories that attempted to "reconcile" the antinomy of self-advancement and class solidarity, he also wrote about the laboring hero who "resist[s] the lure of the ladder" altogether. When enterprising capitalists do appear on the stage of the workingman's tale, as in an Albert Aiken serialized story about the "Molly Maguires," the author "defend[s] the republican community" of striking workers "against the greed of 'self-made men.'"[22] James J. Davis's *The Iron Puddler* (1922), the autobiography of an enterprising wage laborer, reads according to the conventions of the working-class dime novel. For example, the forty-eight-year-old Davis deliberately opens his autobiography with an account of a fistfight between the town bully and himself at age eighteen. "A fight in the first chapter made a book interesting to me when I was a boy," the author recollects.[23] Denning draws a parallel between Davis's opening and the "fistic duel" that typically begins working-class dime novels, such as Whittaker's 1883 tale of Larry Locke, "boy of iron." This type of "structuring event" was deployed in these stories to confer manliness upon their working-class heroes.[24]

I propose to read Davis's enterprising autobiography for what it is not: namely, a middle-class narrative of upward mobility that utilizes the moral luck and market pluck formula. The bulk of *The Iron Puddler* is devoted to the efficacy of hard work and fraternity among wage earners in the mills during the last decades of the nineteenth century. After emigrating from Wales in 1881 at the age of seven, Davis spent the next fifteen years of his life searching for steady work. Like young Andrew Carnegie and Ragged Dick, Davis began working part-time as a telegraph messenger and a bootblack. He secured his first "regular job" sorting nails in a nail factory. Unlike Carnegie, Davis found fraternity rather than fear and loneliness on the factory floor. At age twelve, he was baptized into the exhilarating fires of the iron mill as a master puddler's helper. By age eighteen, he became a master puddler, a trade he eventually used to secure employment in a tin factory.

No Alger boy-hero, the poorly clad, eleven-year-old Jim Davis is given a new blue serge suit by a local charity only to return it at the request of his mother (21). From just such an experience the author generates an antiluck motto promoted throughout his auto-biography: "expect no gift from life" (30). In fact, the fight with the town bully that opens *The Iron Puddler* is motivated by the signifi-cance of the blue suit to Davis's working-class identity. After return-ing the clothes to the charity from which they came, young Jimmy buys a cheap piece of fabric with his hard-earned pennies and gives it to his mother to sew into an ill-fitting suit. When the town bully spies his unevenly stitched garments, he teases Davis: "This was the first time that my spirit had been hurt. His words were a torment that left a scar upon my very soul" (23). When the working boy is fi-nally given an opportunity to fight the bully, he not only gives him a beating but informs him:

> Where you made your mistake was when you made fun of my breeches, seven years ago. And do you remember that blue suit you had on at the time? I know where you got that blue suit of clothes, and I know who had it before you got it. If you still think that a bully in charity clothes can make fun of a boy in clothes that he earned with his own labor, just say so, and I'll give you another clout that will finish you. (25)

Davis's battle with the town bully reverses Ragged Dick's scuffle with his antagonist, Mickey Maguire, who also dons a set of clothes pre-viously worn by his rival. Whereas divine intervention in the form of good fortune allows Dick to ascend from begrimed street urchin to fashionable white-collar office boy, Jimmy refuses to trade his working-class identity for middle-class respectability even if it means maintaining his patchwork garb and eschewing finery.

The Alger formula, which couples moral luck with market pluck, is absent from Davis's working-class story. In *The Iron Puddler* the concept of luck is tied not to personal fortune but, rather, national pride: "Work is a blessing, not a curse. This country had the good luck to be settled by the hardest workers in the world" (269). Here, luck is not the moral agent of individual advancement but, instead, the product of virtuous work performed by the laboring classes. In 1922, Davis, as the newly appointed secretary of labor under President Warren Harding, was authorized in his autobiography to draw the close connection between the U.S. nation and the workingman. The cabinet post also afforded him a forum from which to voice his nativist attitude toward immigrants from outside northern Europe. Nativism, usually wrapped in the banner of Nordicism, was reaching the height of its popularity in America during the early twenties. In this climate, Davis could promote an immigration restriction policy based on fixed racial hierarchies. In a statement directed to U.S. employers and published in 1923 in the journal *Industrial Management*, he advocated reducing immigration into America in order to "protect" the nation from contamination from nonnorthern European nations. "America has always prided itself upon having for its basic stock the so-called 'Nordic races,'" remarks the labor secretary. He adds that it is "shortsighted" to seek cheap labor by welcoming "low grade" immigrants to our shores. "It has been my experience since the days when I worked in the mills," he concludes, "that cheap labor is expensive labor, both for the industry which employs it, and for the community which houses it."[25]

In *The Iron Puddler*, Davis begins from the assumption that "racial characteristics do not change" and argues that, while some races have "good traits" which will help "buil[d] up" America, others have "swinish traits" fit only to "destroy[ing]" the nation (28). He exploits the metaphor of iron puddling in his autobiography to develop his racist argument for denying immigration to lesser breeds:

Some races are pig-iron; Hottentots and Bushmen are pig-iron. They break at a blow. They have been smelted out of wild animalism, but they went no further; they are of no use in this modern world because they are brittle. Only the wrought-iron races can do the work. All this I felt but could not say in the days when I piled the pig-iron in the puddling furnace and turned with boyish eagerness to have my father show me how. (97–98)

The proliferation of nativist attitudes during the twenties (to which I will return in greater detail in chapters 4 and 5) licensed Davis's belief that immigration policy should test for racial purity. The author's attack on non-Nordic immigrants finds an allied cause in his advocacy of the deportation of anarchists and communists, most of whom were believed to be recent arrivals from southern and eastern Europe.

If Davis criticizes communists for promulgating the idea that immoral luck is a factor in business enterprise ("They believe the successful men lack intellect; are all luck" [127]), he also steadfastly refuses to use the Algeresque concept of ethical good fortune in explaining self-advancement. Instead, Davis promotes the character-based virtues of thrift and hard work when, for example, he reflects on the rags-to-riches achievements of entrepreneurs from his boyhood hometown of Sheron, Pennsylvania:

I learned that the banker, the hotel keeper and the station agent had all been poor boys like myself. They started with nothing but their hands to labor with. They had worked hard and saved a part of their wages, and this had given them "a start." . . . From this I learned that laborers became capitalists when they saved their money. (76–77)

Neither does Davis deploy the language of luck to explain his personal triumphs when hard work and thrift will do. He insists that, as a poor boy on the factory floor, he "lusted" for labor: "I worked and I liked it" (87). Late in *The Iron Puddler*, the reader learns that the author went "from tin worker to small capitalist" not by becoming a captain of industry but by possessing the good business sense to save money and invest it wisely (240).

Davis's greatest achievement comes when, after securing employment in a tin factory at age twenty-two, he rallies his coworkers to vote against an imprudent strike. As a result, he is elected president of his local union, the Amalgamated Association of Iron, Steel and Tin Workers of North America. Davis acknowledges that his reputation for resolving disputes between labor and capital through negotiated compromise coupled with a "thorough knowledge of the production end of the business" opened doors for him "to get out of the labor field and into the field of management." However, he declined these opportunities, explaining that not only was he unfamiliar with "salesmanship" as an occupation but that he felt a "natural feeling of fraternity" among workingmen (207).

2

Gender Stability

Troubling the Horatio Alger Formula: *Tattered Tom*

Women, like working-class men, rarely occupy center stage in the copious "luck and pluck" stories. The only exception is Alger's *Tattered Tom; or, The Story of a Street Arab*, where the boy-hero is, in fact, a heroine. Tom, a street sweep in New York City, cross-dresses in order to create and sustain a masculine identity. Her cross-dressing splits the self-identical subject of manly enterprise and exposes it as a social construction. However, the cult of true womanhood ultimately thwarts Tom's efforts to sustain a masculine identity. The power of domestic ideology frustrates her participation in what Michael Moon labels the male homosocial market economy of late Victorian society.[1] In the end, Alger's fiction recuperates the domestic ideal by leaving in tatters Tom's dream of autonomous public sphere participation and advancement.

If, as discussed earlier, clothing is a preeminent sign of success in rags-to-riches stories, fashion takes on heightened significance in *Tattered Tom*. Here, the twelve-year-old hero(ine) is initially identified as a "bundle of rags" by a gentleman considered to be "a leader of fashion." It is left to the story's narrator to sort through the begrimed bundle in search of its proper identity: "It was not quite easy to determine whether it was a boy or a girl. The head was surmounted by a boy's cap, the hair was cut short, it wore a boy's jacket, but underneath was a girl's dress."[2] The reader is told in the opening pages that the protagonist is not a true Tom but a tomboy. However, the narrator's use of the gender neutral pronoun "it" in the initial description of the protagonist is reinforced by onlookers who repeatedly view Tom as a "strange creature—half boy in appearance" (42–43). Early on, the reader learns that, on the menacing streets of New York, "Tom claimed no immunity or privilege on the score of sex." She recognizes that her independence is based on her ability to maintain a masculine identity in the public marketplace, and thus she desires to be a boy. In fact, she "regarded herself, to all intents and purposes, as a boy, and strongly wished that she were one" (55–56).

Tom is not immune to the moral luck that propels the Alger hero up the ladder of success. However, because this sort of middle-class respectability compels her to desire the domestic ideal, it is unclear whether moral luck for an enterprising woman is a gift or a life sentence. Just at the moment when the reader learns that "Tom, like others of her sex, found herself shut out from an employment for which she considered herself fitted" (71), good fortune is bestowed in the form of a warmhearted Christian named Albert Barnes, who takes it upon himself to "civilize" the "untamed" girl (72). "There's enough in her to make a very smart woman," he thinks, "if she is placed under the right influences and properly trained" (90). As Alger's colleague, Christian reformer Charles Loring Brace of the Children's Aid Society, insisted, nothing enriches the respectable character of young women like industrious housework.[3] In this spirit, Barnes turns Tom over to his sister, Martha Merton, who runs a boardinghouse. In a chapter titled "Tom Drops Her Tatters," Martha begins her instruction in domesticity by giving Tom feminine attire and insisting that she use her "real name," Jenny. Finally, Tom "ceased to be a street Arab, and obtained a respectable home" (139).

Her new life is momentarily interrupted when she is wrongly accused of the most heinous sin in the Alger lexicon, dishonesty. The content of her character is directly challenged. Without a moral rudder to guide her, Tom returns to the streets. However, her newly acquired feminine identity, like her new attire, is not shed so easily in her old environment. Offered the opportunity to sweep sidewalks, she refuses because she perceives that the task is "too dirty" (201). Street sweeping is, for a finely clad young lady with higher aspirations, a shameful occupation. Moral luck returns to Tom when, by divine grace, her wealthy and forgotten mother finally finds her long-lost daughter. The story concludes with the establishment of the protagonist's proper surname, Jane Lindsay, along with the narrator's assurance that "the influence of an excellent mother will, I am convinced, in time eradicate" all traces of *Tattered Tom* (275). In Andrew Carnegie's autobiography, symbolic orphan status offered a way to wealth. In Alger's only female "luck and pluck" story, the domestic influence of a mother simultaneously secures Tom's place within the home and forecloses opportunities for her public sphere ambitions.

True Womanhood in the Market: Harriet Hubbard Ayer

Middle-class women's assignment to domestic space diminished their access to the world of business enterprise. In fact, their relation to the marketplace was usually of a disinterested sort. Because women took on the roles of virtuous mothers and supporting wives, entrepreneurial success was mediated through the achievements of men. Throughout the nineteenth century and beyond, it was the task of the good wife or mother to nurture a husband's or a son's sense of virtue. As Wyllie points out, the aspiring businessman chose his wife not on the basis of her financial worth but because the "good wife enriched her husband by bringing profitable qualities of character, not money, into the home."[4] However, when independent women entered the masculine arena of free enterprise, they not only abandoned their role as domestic guardian of character. They also pioneered many of the consumer-oriented personality industries, such as cosmetics, which mass-marketed the beautification of women that helped to undermine some of the protocols of true womanhood.

It is important to remember, as Caroline Bird's historical survey of female entrepreneurs demonstrates, that women who have been at the forefront of business ventures rarely have led rags-to-riches lives. If the enterprising woman was not born into wealth, then she usually married into it.[5] More commonly than not, women became entrepreneurs only after a matrimonial crisis, such as the death or divorce of a husband. Their marketplace ambitions typically led to the diminishment of their domestic authority as wives or mothers. The life of Harriet Hubbard Ayer, a pioneering cosmetic entrepreneur in the last decades of the nineteenth century, is a case in point. Her story illustrates how the domestic ideal not only worked to obstruct women's activity within the marketplace but also delegitimated the female entrepreneur's domestic authority as wife or mother.

Ayer's experiences offer a prominent example of a riches-to-rags-to-riches pattern not uncommon among enterprising women of the late nineteenth century. Her story is unusual in that she left autobiographical statements, albeit in the form of advertisements for the company that bore her name. Like most women, Ayer got her business start only by first gaining autonomy from the male authority figure in her life. Perhaps unlike many of these women, Ayer initiated her own path to independence by divorcing her husband of seventeen years during the mid-1880s. This began a series of sensational legal battles, played out in the popular press as well as in the courts, that lasted for fifteen years. Civil suits filed against Ayer focused on three issues: her suitability for child custody, her competency in managing a corporation, and her sanity. The legal challenges to Ayer's authority in the private and the public spheres constituted attempts to maintain residual notions of true womanhood in the face of expanding business opportunities for female entrepreneurs.

In contrast to the legend of the self-made man, Harriet Ayer's life began at the top of the social ladder.[6] Her father made a fortune in real estate; her husband, Herbert Copeland Ayer, whom she wed in 1865 at age sixteen, inherited a prosperous Ohio iron dealership, Brown, Bunnell & Co., from his father and became a leading Chicago business executive. Harriet, now married, lived a life of leisure while managing her husband's home and cultivating an interest in European decorative arts. She also developed, from a comfortable distance, an interest in the rights of labor and women's suffrage. In 1882, estranged from her husband, she left Chicago for New York with her two daughters. A year later, her husband's financial empire collapsed, and the once wealthy society matron was now a divorcée and unable to sustain the privileged lifestyle to which she was accustomed.

Determined not to allow the end of her marriage and decline in financial security to ruin her life or that of her children, Ayer found employment as a saleswoman in an exclusive New York furniture establishment, Sypher & Co., which catered to wealthy women. According to newspaper reports, Harriet Ayer was hired because Sypher & Co. felt that she—a woman of character who had fallen on hard times—would attract customers. Before beginning work, Ayer felt compelled to explain her unorthodox behavior to her husband via a letter to one of his close associates: "As your opinion has great weight with Mr. Ayer, will you as a great favor to me take my part when he explodes as he will, about my going to work. . . . When Mr. A. is able to set aside a sum of money upon the income on which we can live, I shall be willing to fold my hands."[7] Although she was successful as a saleswoman, Harriet Ayer did not earn a fortune off her commissions. In the midst of a front-page story in the *New York Times* a decade later (on the topic of her ex-husband's attempt to have her permanently committed to an insane asylum), the reporter sketched her early success at Sypher & Co. in this manner: "She soon succeeded in building up a large clientele. . . . She was apparently born with a genius for business, and for several years it was estimated that she was making from $10,000 to $15,000 per annum."[8] During these years, Ayer found herself traveling throughout Europe to hunt down antiques for customers.

It was on just such a trip in 1886 that Ayer later claimed to have purchased the Récamier formula from M. Mirault, a transaction that opened the door to free enterprise. Mirault's grandfather, a Parisian chemist, reportedly made the cream that kept the skin of the famous Madame Récamier (according to legend, a woman Napoléon feared because of her beauty) youthful well beyond her prime. In order to buy the skin-care formula from Mirault, Ayer was forced to go to a family friend and Wall Street broker, James Seymour, for fifty thousand dollars. As we will see, three years later this sum of money sparked a civil suit in which Seymour claimed the amount was an investment, which gave him control over the company, whereas Ayer maintained that it was a loan previously repaid. Ayer patented and began to market her skin-care medicine in April 1887, just when

American women were starting to use specialized cosmetics to aid their complexion.

Going into business for oneself was a bold move for a woman of the late nineteenth century. Ayer's most daring and innovative stroke lay in the manner in which she marketed her product: she offered her own name and the Hubbard coat of arms for the Récamier trademark. This promotional ploy symbolically situated Ayer, as a woman previously assigned to the sphere of domesticity and leisure, within the manly marketplace. In late-Victorian America, however, using a woman's name to sell a product was considered outside the bounds of good taste. Nevertheless, this marketing strategy coupled with Ayer's literary flair for creating appealing advertisement copy generated strong sales in England as well as the United States. Her advertising acumen extended to a daring appropriation of the figure of the self-made man for herself. In a booklet advertising her line of cosmetics, she wove her own riches-to-rags-to-riches story into a sales pitch. Ayer tells of traveling in France as a wealthy man's wife when, suffering from sunburn, she obtains a salve from a once-prominent countess who consents to sell her the Récamier formula.

> In those days I was a rich woman. I little dreamed that the scrap of paper which contained the directions for an old French skin preservative would be the keystone to a gigantic business. So it proved, for when I found myself absolutely penniless, and in order to support myself and educate my children, I obtained a position in a large bric-a-brac house in New York, often working very late at night. . . . [I was] a woman without a dollar beyond the wages earned by [my] head and hands.[9]

The advertisement introduces a family physician who diagnoses Ayer's faltering health as work-related stress. Nevertheless he is moved to make the following compliment: "Mrs. Ayer, how in the world do you keep your skin so smooth and fair in spite of loss of sleep, lack of proper exercise and irregular meals? What do you use for your complexion?" Ayer reveals the skin cream's ingredients to the doctor. The physician not only gives his scientific blessing to the skin-care formula but also advises his patient to sell the product so that other women may also benefit from its wonders. "From this conversation,"

Ayer concludes, "I date the inception of the business which is now known all over the world."

Advertisements are not conventional autobiographical source material. However, in the case of nontraditional entrepreneurs, where no authoritative self-composition exists, I have found it necessary to utilize unorthodox evidence. Ayer's advertisement, in particular, illustrates how privileged white women in the late nineteenth century might have appropriated and rewritten an enterprising narrative for themselves. The absence of Ayer's divorce from the ad copy is symptomatic of the range of representation appropriate to a female uplift story. First, she performs a reversal of the rags-to-riches story. Her self-promoting portrait moves abruptly from her days as "a rich woman" to the moment when she finds herself "absolutely penniless." Second, her ambition is represented in terms of disinterested domestic values, which allows Ayer to maintain her status as a good wife and mother. Finally, although her father and husband are both absent from the ad, her personal ambition is authorized through the paternal advice of the family physician. In another advertisement for Récamier, which appeared in the *New York World*, Ayer describes the satisfaction the product gave her high-class customers. The promotional campaign includes a list of prominent family names of "well-known society women," including "the Vanderbilt, Astor, Kernochan, Goelet, Lorillard, Beckwith—in fact, every one of the most aristocratic families of old New York."[10] These advertisements functioned to confer the seal of high-society respectability on Ayer and, by implication, on her mass-marketed cosmetics.

Ayer's success, however, was short-lived. As the 1880s came to a close, her fortunes took a turn for the worse when Jim Seymour (previously a friend, business associate, and now father-in-law to her eldest daughter) brought a lawsuit against her. He charged, as a stockholder in Récamier Preparations, that not only was Ayer mismanaging the company's operations but she was mentally ill. The sensation aroused by his accusations and by Ayer's countersuit made newspaper headlines in the spring of 1889. According to Ayer's sworn testimony, the conspirator attempted to deprive her of her mental health by having a doctor prescribe a debilitating drug. She claimed that

Seymour's intent was to incapacitate her and, in doing so, to gain control of the company.

In the popular press, an attention to matters of sexual impropriety overwhelmed what might, in a different context, have been reported as a business dispute between two enterprising individuals. A *New York Herald* story, for instance, reported the case in sensational detail. Under the headline "Crazed by Drugs—Left at Death's Door," the story opens:

> Never outside of the realms of romance was a more dramatic story told than was set forth in the affidavits read before Judge Daly, in the court of Common Pleas, yesterday. A woman whose success in business has made her name familiar in every town and city from the Atlantic Ocean to the Pacific, charged a stockbroker, a man whose wealth is estimated at many millions, with a crime that appears almost incredible in this century. . . . In order to rob her of her money these people [Seymour and his coconspirators], according to her sworn assertions, wished to have her declared insane and placed in an asylum.[11]

The newspaper account leaves no doubt as to Ayer's self-made success. However, in the same article the *Herald* published seven letters, provided by Jim Seymour, which Ayer immediately dismissed as forgeries. They were signed by both Margaret, Ayer's youngest daughter, and her governess, Blanche Howard, and they were addressed to Ayer's other daughter, Hattie.

The published correspondence is important less because of its reliability as truthful documentation (the fact that Seymour's attorneys decided against entering the letters as evidence in court suggests that they were forged) than for what it reveals about the social climate under which an independent businesswoman such as Ayer labored. Seymour's case against her depended on his ability to exploit conventional assumptions about a woman's proper role. Ayer's transgressions against femininity could best be documented not through the testimony of businessmen but by those who challenged her authority in the home: her daughters and their governess. It was one thing to charge Ayer with alcoholism and insanity but it was quite another to link such weaknesses to the performance of her domestic duties. In a letter to Hattie, dated 25 January 1889, and published in the *Herald*, Margaret accuses her mother not only of lying but of being an "awfully bad woman" who is addicted to habits that make everyone hate her. "How I wish our mother was good. It's awful, and the only thing we can do is to try and make ourselves as much unlike her as we can." Margaret concludes her letter with two additional barbs meant to delegitimate her mother's claim to the mantle of femininity: "I don't think she is pretty either, for if you ever got all the paint, rouge, whitewash and dye off (but you never will) you'd see she was much different than you thought she was. I think it was very mean of her to leave Papa as soon as he lost his money."[12] As a matter of fact, Harriet left her husband prior to his financial ruin. Nevertheless, a published statement made by a twelve-year-old accusing her mother of dishonesty, a bad temperament, cheap vanity, and matrimonial unfaithfulness transformed a business dispute into a public hearing on the fledgling culture of consumption. The published letters were an implicit indictment not only of the female entrepreneurs responsible for producing mass-marketed cosmetics but of the women who consumed them. The *Herald* thus offered a forum for those who believed that consumerism and the manufacture of products for the new consumer markets demeaned women and jeopardized the moral lives of those who came under their care.

One week later, newspapers reported that Ayer's lawyers had little difficulty revealing the blatant contradictions and lies in Seymour's accusations.[13] Her reputation and that of the product that carried her name, however, were irreparably damaged by the notoriety aroused in the popular press. If this was not difficult enough for Ayer, a month after the trial ended, her ex-husband, Herbert, asked a Chicago court for an injunction to restrain Harriet from maintaining custody of Margaret (Hattie was now married). Some evidence previously dismissed in the trial over business dealings with Seymour was allowed in the court battle over child custody with her ex-husband. As the *New York Times* later reported: "He charged that his wife [*sic*] was an unfit person to look after the girl; that she had become addicted to the use of morphine and alcohol, . . . and that she was not a moral woman."[14] Although the custody hearing was conducted "behind closed doors," testimony that linked Ayer's name to prominent politicians and businessmen was leaked to the press. The *Times* suggests that these unspoken charges were enough to give custody of Margaret to her father.[15] This was a court battle that Harriet Ayer could not win. Although enterprising men might be accepted in the public eye after being found guilty of poor judgment or even recklessness in personal affairs, the sexual double standard ensured that the same leniency would not be afforded to businesswomen who might also be wives or mothers.[16] For Ayer, the price of short-lived marketplace success was the loss of moral authority in her domestic life.

There is a postscript to this phase of Harriet Ayer's public life that is worth mentioning. In 1893, those apparently conspiring against Ayer were finally successful in placing her—against her will—in an insane asylum. With assistance from her lawyers, she was able to secure her release fourteen months later. Afterward, she agitated against the institutional treatment of the insane and those thought to be mentally ill. As her own cosmetics business sputtered during this period, Ayer found another way of maintaining influence within the fledgling personality-enhancing industries. In 1896, she took a position as a *New York World* columnist, where she offered health and beauty advice for the newly inaugurated woman's page of the Sunday edition.

Domesticating Business: The "Emma McChesney" Trilogy

Despite the gender barrier faced by women within the male marketplace, the literary imagination was one arena in which a middle-class woman of uncompromised moral standing might achieve more than momentary success. At the height of the Progressive Era, popular novelist Edna Ferber (remembered today as the author of *Giant*) presented just such an enterprising heroine in the form of the beloved Emma McChesney, a divorcée and single parent. Emma's unorthodox ambitions are prompted by necessity. The reader learns that she is the victim of an alcoholic husband who failed to provide for his family. Emma divorces him and, at the time she lands a job with T. A. Buck Featherloom Petticoat and Lingerie Company, is "penniless, refusing support from the man she had married eight years before." Her employer "watche[s] her rise" from typist to traveling sales representative for the coveted Midwest territory.[17] Even more impressive is the fact that, in twelve short years, Emma "had risen from the humble position of stenographer . . . to the secretaryship of the firm."[18]

The "Emma McChesney" trilogy—consisting of *Roast Beef, Medium* (1913), *Personality Plus* (1914), and *Emma McChesney & Co.* (1915)—inaugurated a hybrid literary form: the domestic business novel. Ferber's popular stories incorporated the middle-class moralism of nineteenth-century domestic fiction (which, as Nancy Armstrong argues, was authorized by a social contract that enforced separate spheres)[19] into the burgeoning business novel format. The trilogy, initially serialized in *American Magazine*, offered working- and middle-class women readers a fantasy escape from what were more often than not boring, dead-end jobs in and outside the home. Through her heroine, Emma McChesney, the author attempted to resolve the contradiction for enterprising women who wished to remain faithful to the ideals of true womanhood.

Ferber imagines a female subjectivity capable of mastering men's business without forfeiting the domestic virtues assigned to femininity. Her "lady drummer" brings domesticity to bear upon the unscrupulous world of cutthroat sales competition. In the end, Emma's actions do less to undermine the separation of gendered spheres than to give cultural authority to the domestic ideal within a narrative of enterprise. Although Ferber's saleswoman insists from the very beginning that "Any place in the world is the place for a lady" and "Any work is woman's work that a woman can do well" (*RB*, 67, 258), she is portrayed as an exception rather than the rule among women.[20] Emma repeatedly runs into men who are aghast at the idea of an independent woman on the road selling goods. "A man just naturally refuses to talk business to a pretty woman," an advertising executive pronounces. In the same breath, however, he concedes that Emma is "one woman in a million" (*PP*, 52). In the employ of the Featherloom company, she is "known from coast to coast as the most successful traveling saleswoman in the business."[21] She has all the market pluck of the traditional self-made man—sagacity and self-control, confidence and commitment, practicality and perseverance—and more. She declares:

> T. A. Buck's Featherloom Petticoats have been my existence for almost ten years. I've sold Featherlooms six days in the week, and seven when I had a Sunday customer. They've not only been my business and my means of earning a livelihood, they've been my religion, my diversion, my life, my pet pastime. I've lived petticoats, I've talked petticoats, I've sold petticoats, I've dreamed petticoats—why, I've even worn the darned things! And that's more than any man will ever do. (*RB*, 156)

Emma is not merely a drummer peddling her company's wares. As a woman, she has a firsthand knowledge of the product and its consumer.

Between 1880 and 1920, as an abundance of commodities generated the need for expanded markets, enterprising women found their earliest and most profitable opportunities for autonomous self-making within the sector of the economy that catered to their newly created consumer desires. This is reflected in the opening chapter of *The Girl and the Job* (1919), where authors Helen Hoerle and Florence Saltzberg advise young women that there exist "many things that girls may sell profitably," most notably "those that we are most familiar with . . . cooked food, clothes, and flowers."[22] Hoerle and Saltzberg insist that although traveling salesmanship may be a fickle occupation, it need not be gender-bound.[23] Curiously enough, when it comes time to locate a convincing example of a successful saleswoman capable of overturning the stereotype of the male drummer, the authors turn to Ferber's fictional heroine:

> The work of the commercial traveler is well illustrated in the stories of the well-known author, Edna Ferber. She has turned out the most readable fiction on what work as a drummer may mean to a woman in the way of joy and sorrow, trouble and pleasure. How one woman managed to maintain a womanly and dignified bearing, and at the same time a bright and engaging cordiality of manner; how she managed to keep in good health under conditions so trying that many men fail to do so; how she managed not only to earn a good living for herself, but also for her son whom she sent to college—any girl who is thinking of becoming a drummer should read.[24]

This example illustrates how popular fiction has the power to generate models for enterprise where, in actuality, none exists. The "Emma McChesney" trilogy produced the conditions by which a working girl might imagine herself on the most revered and manly terrain in America: the open road. The *New York Times*, in a review of *Emma McChesney & Co.*, had recognized the achievement of Ferber's heroine when they crowned her "a defier of precedent" and "the pioneer among traveling saleswomen."[25] Hoerle and Saltzberg explicitly instruct the working girl who wants to become a drummer to ask herself, "Could I be another Emma McChesney?"[26] The example on which they draw suggests the manner in which the popular formulas reproduced in success literature from Alger to Ferber helped shape the actual lives of individuals.

Emma's capacity to uphold her domestic duties despite her entrepreneurial adventures was confirmed by one reviewer for the *New York Times* who dubbed her a "plucky mother."[27] Personal advancement is, in the first instance, the objective of the self-made man. In the case of Ferber's heroine, however, the welfare of her seventeen-year-old son, Jock, is always at the forefront of her career ambitions: "Those ten years on the road! . . . And all for Jock" (*PP*, 151). Emma's success seems to be the by-product of her "maternal instinct" (*RB*, 13) and of "self-denial for her son Jock" (*EM*, 62). "Next to my boy at school," she tells her boss, the firm is "the biggest thing in my life" (*RB*, 258). Ferber does not include moral luck in the recipe for Emma's rise. Rather, as the authors of *The Girl and the Job* recognize, the virtues of true womanhood that Emma brings to her occupation—dignity, cordiality, good health, and maternal sacrifice—create the conditions for her success.

But Emma brings another quality to the maturing consumer marketplace, namely, personality. Philosophers of success warned against an excess of personality, for which they thought women to be particularly prone. An ad man in Ferber's fiction, immediately after explaining the role of personality in modern business methods, offers a warning about the damage that an unharnessed personality can do to sales. His illustration takes the form of an overwrought female employee: "Look at Miss Galt. When we have a job that needs a woman's eye do we send her? No. Why? Because she's too blame charming. Too much personality" (*PP*, 51–52). Alternatively, Mrs. McChesney is tops in sales because she knows how to exploit her personality for optimum efficiency and effectiveness. Even her rival Fat Ed Meyers concedes that her success is based not on her petticoats but on her "personality" (*EM*, 42).

Even by the standards of their contemporaries, there was one quality that neither Ferber nor her heroine expressly possessed: feminism.[28] Still, some of Ferber's avid readers were skeptical about a woman's capacity to maintain traditional female virtues after being exposed to the rough-and-tumble world of business enterprise. The most famous fan of Ferber's Bull Moose heroine was Theodore Roosevelt, who publicly declared his admiration for Emma's spunk and ambition but had trouble squaring her successful career with her choice to forgo the institution of marriage. Although Roosevelt was quoted in the press as commending the author for "the way in which Mrs. McChesney solves her sociological problems,"[29] he was decidedly less enthusiastic about Emma's resistance to matrimony. In the December 1912 issue of *American Magazine*, an advertisement for one of Ferber's "Emma McChesney" stories trumpeted: "In the heat of his [presidential] campaign, Colonel Roosevelt wrote a characteristic letter to Miss Ferber, part protest, part appeal and part command that Emma McChesney *get married at once!*"[30]

Ferber was as strong-willed as her fictional heroine. In advertising the upcoming "Emma McChesney" stories, the editor of *American Magazine* reluctantly informed his readers: "Emma McChesney . . . positively refuses to marry T. A. Buck. The pleading of Miss Ferber, even the insistence of Colonel Roosevelt . . . was without effect."[31] Prior to publishing the final volume of the trilogy in 1915, the author resisted the injunctions of Roosevelt and her editor. Ferber recognized that marriage meant the end to her enterprising heroine as her readers knew her. She had grander plans for the self-proclaimed "lady captain of finance" (*RB*, 269). At the outset of *Emma McChesney & Co.*, Emma all but conquers the corporate hierarchy. Although second in command to T. A. Buck Jr. (the attractive but ineffectual son of the original and now deceased T. A. Buck, founder of Featherloom), Emma runs the day-to-day operations of the firm with the efficiency of the most conscientious homemaker. "But now comes her greatest exploit," raved the *New York Times*.[32] Our heroine risks her reputation for irreproachable business instincts, not to mention the financial stability of the firm, on a scheme designed to open up the company's sales territory abroad. Emma's enterprising expedition in South American markets pushes to the limit the contradiction of the true woman in the business world. Ferber strives to resolve this inconsistency by demonstrating the efficient fit between domesticity and free enterprise. After four months abroad, Emma returns home "gloriously triumphant." Over the inept protest of the company president and romantic love-interest, T. A. Buck, she "had invaded the southern continent and left it abloom with Featherlooms from the Plata to the Canal" (*EM*, 43). Ferber's message seems to be that, even as Emma's commercial crusade leaves Latin America littered with corsets, her heroine's feminine touch beautifies the continent. Emma's success confirms the profitability of female enterprise in the postfrontier nation.

Emma's commercial victory abroad does less to legitimate her agency within the business world than to sanction her influence in the public sphere. As she navigates her way through South American markets, her industrious example inspires (or perhaps shames) T. A. Buck into making himself a man by asserting his entrepreneurial authority at home. Traveling as a salesman throughout Emma's old territory, the American Midwest, not only reinvigorates T. A.; it also lays the groundwork for Emma's reentry into domesticity by means of marriage to the company boss. This signals what Ferber calls, with a wink and a nod, "a closer corporation." However, it is a business merger that differently affects husband and wife. The enterprising achievements of Emma Buck are incorporated into the domestic economy. The closing novel in the trilogy tries to persuade the reader that Emma's greatest success is not her rise in retail but the feminine influence she exercises over the men in her life. Her fiancé expresses his gratitude with reference to her womanly capacity to nurture others: "And what I am to-day you have made me, directly and indirectly, by association and by actual orders, by suggestion, and by direct contact. What you did for Jock, purposefully and by force, you did for me, too. . . . you've made—actually made, molded shaped, and turned out two men" (*EM*, 92). As this passage suggests, the expansion of domestic influence into the world of business denies women agency within the market economy.

In the end, the popular trilogy maintained the efficacy of separate spheres for men and women. Emma never recovers the autonomy and authority that made her the most renowned saleswoman in Ferber's America. She is also complicit in her own retirement from entrepreneurial activity as she sacrifices her famous personality at the altar: "She learned to efface her own personality that others might shine who had a better right" (*EM*, 228). She dutifully, if reluctantly, throws off the mantle of self-making in order to fulfill her proper role as Mrs. Buck, who brings moral integrity to her husband's ambition. The final installment in the trilogy illustrates the extent to which the residual concept of moral character is not confined to the masculinist success literature of Horatio Alger. It extends as well to the fiction of Edna Ferber, where the accomplished self-made woman retreats into the home and, in doing so, maintains traditional gender assignments that were undergoing imminent change.

3

Racial Segregation

The Political Economy of a Lynch Mob:
Tom Moss, Calvin McDowell, and Henry Stewart

Marketplace segregation was the most severe restraint placed on black entrepreneurship at the turn of the twentieth century. It left many African Americans wondering whether or not Jim Crow truly had the opportunity to become a self-made man. The issue was at the heart of an 1899 publication titled *The Negro in Business*, the first systematic investigation of black enterprise in the United States. The book's editor, W. E. B. Du Bois, opened the Atlanta University study by insisting that it was impossible "to place too great stress on the deep significance of business ventures among American Negroes. Physical emancipation came in 1863, but economic emancipation is still far off."[1] Statistics amassed in *The Negro in Business* point to approximately five thousand black Americans engaged in private businesses during the last decade of the nineteenth century.[2] Few of these black enterprises manufactured industrial goods. Most, like Madam C. J. Walker's cosmetics company, were concentrated in the consumer-oriented service and retail sectors of the segregated economy. "These enterprises," Du Bois concluded, "are peculiar instances of the 'advantage of the disadvantage'—of the way in which a hostile environment has forced the Negro to do for himself."[3]

Black entrepreneurs, attentive to generating the conditions under which their investments might flourish, actively incorporated the imposition of segregation into the very fabric of their business schemes. This exploitation of the preassigned color-coded markets was a strategy of economic survival that was supported by the majority of black intellectuals and race leaders. The Atlanta University study, for example, adopted the following resolution: "The mass of the Negroes must learn to patronize business enterprises conducted by their own race, even at some slight disadvantage."[4] The resolution's reference to "some slight disadvantage" suggests the limits of individual enterprise as well as the importance of racial solidarity within segregated America.

The yoke of segregation extended well beyond the problem of patronage. The disadvantage might also lead to death when white entrepreneurs operating in black communities felt their businesses threatened by black-owned shops. Journalist Ida B. Wells, an enterprising individual in her own right, discovered in the last decade of the nineteenth century that white commerce and civic leaders exploited every means available—including lynching—to discourage the development of Negro businesses. In her autobiography, Wells reports that her thirty-year "crusade for justice" was originally based on a fundamental discovery: lynching was primarily motivated by the threat black access to free enterprise posed to white entrepreneurs. It was an "excuse," she insisted, "to get rid of Negroes who were acquiring wealth and property and thus keep the race terrorized and 'keep the nigger down.'"[5]

In her posthumously published autobiography, originally composed between 1928 and 1931, Wells presents herself as an independent-minded black woman. Her familiarity with stories of the self-made man in America was initiated by her extensive childhood reading list, which included Oliver Optic's Algeresque stories for boyhood uplift alongside both Western classics and domestic fiction for little women.[6] As an adult, her career as a militant black reporter flourished despite numerous obstacles, including the threat of lynching from angry whites. Nevertheless, her memoirs consistently undersell what she calls her "little success" in the arena of activist journalism.[7]

In March 1892, just prior to her thirtieth birthday, Wells observed a lynching in Memphis, which she contends "changed the whole course of my life."[8] While living in Memphis and editing the city's black newspaper, *Free Speech*, a close friend named Thomas Moss, along with Calvin McDowell and Henry Stewart, was lynched by a white mob. These men were respected entrepreneurs within the segregated Tennessee community in which they resided. "All of them were engaged in the mercantile business," states Wells in *A Red Record*, a pamphlet cataloging the truth about lynching. All, according to the author's account, "were known to be among the most honorable, reliable, worthy and peaceable colored citizens of the community."[9] In regard to her friend Tom Moss, who was the principal investor in the black-owned and -operated People's Grocery Company, Wells comments: "He owned his little home, and having saved his money he went into the grocery business with the same ambition that a young white man would have had."[10] People's Grocery was in direct competition with an establishment across the street owned by a white man named Barrett, who had previously had a monopoly on commercial trade in the heavily populated black suburb.[11]

A series of provocations by Barrett and his associates resulted in a Saturday night assault on People's Grocery. Black men gathered in the store and armed themselves for the anticipated confrontation. During the skirmish, gunfire wounded three white men before their compatriots fled the scene. The Sunday morning headlines whipped the white community into a frenzy by announcing that the wounded were officers of the law who were simply carrying out their duty to arrest criminals supposedly being harbored in the black-owned grocery. Such sensationalism sanctioned law officials to imprison more than one hundred black men. Three days later, during the early morning hours, a group of white men arrived at the local jail. After gaining admittance, they dragged the three officials of People's Grocery out of their cells. Tom Moss, Calvin McDowell, and Henry Stewart were taken a mile out of town and lynched. Soon thereafter a white mob looted their store, forcing its creditors to close the establishment and auction off the remaining stock.

In her newspaper, *Free Speech*, Wells reported Tom Moss's last words to his executioners: "tell my people to go West—there is no justice for them here." The black citizens of Memphis responded. In an effort to pressure white authorities to bring the lynchers to justice, they not only left Memphis in droves but those who remained boycotted white-owned businesses. Wells, who was instrumental in supporting the black exodus and organizing the local boycott, analyzes the circumstances at the opening of a chapter titled "Self Help" in *Southern Horrors* (1892):

> To Northern capital and Afro-American labor the South owes its rehabilitation. If labor is withdrawn capital will not remain. The Afro-American is thus the backbone of the South. A thorough knowledge and judicious exercise of this power in lynching localities could many times effect a bloodless revolution. The white man's dollar is his god, and to stop this will be to stop outrages in many localities.[12]

Wells's keen comprehension of the logic of segregated enterprise allowed her to forge a twofold strategy that effectively addressed both the fears of the white lynchers and the desires of the black community. First, by understanding that God and Mammon walked hand in hand in the mind of Northern investors, Wells appealed to their sense of a higher law by shrewdly aiming at their purse strings. Second, she couched the militant Memphis boycott in the conventional language of self-reliance, concluding the "Self Help" chapter with the proverb: "The gods help those who help themselves."[13] Her community-based self-help activism was enough of a threat to white enterprise that, while she was away in New York a few months later, the office of *Free Speech* was destroyed by prominent white citizens. Friends in Memphis cautioned Wells that she would be in imminent danger from an angry lynch mob if she ever returned to her place of business. The threat only strengthened her steadfast resolve to campaign for justice on behalf of enterprising black Americans.

Wells admits that, prior to the lynching of the three businessmen in Memphis, she had never seriously questioned the officially sanctioned motive behind the white South's frequent lynching of blacks since the Civil War. "Like many another person who had read of lynching in the South," she says, "I had accepted the idea meant to be conveyed—that although lynching was irregular and contrary to law and order, unreasoning anger over the terrible crime of rape led to the lynching." Yet, this alibi did not square with the facts of the Memphis lynching, despite the white newspapers' attempts to use it as a justification in this incident as well. Moss, McDowell, and Stewart had committed no crime against white women. The true story of lynching was not white men protecting the honor of Southern womanhood against the threat of the black rapist. Rather, the tale that needed to be told concerned the license that such an alibi gave whites in their attempt to thwart the efforts of enterprising black men and, in doing so, terrorize the entire African American community.

Free Enterprise: Booker T. Washington

In 1892, the year that Tom Moss, Calvin McDowell, and Henry Stewart were murdered, lynching reached an all-time high.[14] It is the same period in which Booker T. Washington emerged on the national scene. To many, Washington appeared as the traditional self-made man in black. He embraced an individualist ethos founded on the virtues of character-based success. To do so, he turned a blind eye to even the most pernicious forms of American racism, as is evident in a statement that appeared near the beginning of his 1901 autobiography, *Up From Slavery*. He claims that the Ku Klux Klan not only no longer existed but "the fact that such [an organization] ever existed is almost forgotten by both races."[15] It was well known that Washington, who advanced his personal career while attempting to uplift the race, downplayed the occurrence and the significance of Southern lynching throughout his influential career. This helps explain how he could be such an unapologetic advocate for mainstream notions of individual enterprise in a segregated society. Moreover, his accommodationist approach to politics compelled him to urge prospective black businessmen to follow the Protestant work ethic. He went so far as to say that "it is well to bear in mind that whatever other sins the South may be called to bear, when it comes to business, pure and simple, it is in the South that the Negro is given a man's chance in the commercial world" (146–50). Washington masked the deadly white competition encountered by men such as Tom Moss only by adhering strictly to the racially coded narrative of self-making.

It may not be an overstatement to say that *Up From Slavery* was the most widely read book written by a black American in the first half of the twentieth century. Most contemporary reviewers, in the black and white press alike, hailed it as a first-rate achievement and a descendant of a legacy inaugurated by Benjamin Franklin.[16] At the most basic level, Washington's autobiography authorized black uplift through the appropriation of a residual model of American success. Washington, an avid reader of Horatio Alger, was indelibly influenced by the middle-class conception of virtuous enterprise. This elucidates his infamous description of slavery as a "school" (37).[17] By classifying slavery as a precursor to black industrial education, he simply ignored its dogged legacy in the wake of the failure of Reconstruction.

The title of *Up From Slavery* is ambiguous enough to suggest either a rags-to-riches story or a narrative of an ex-bondsman. However, once the reader moves beyond the first chapter, the book focuses not on the significance of slavery and its legacy in industrial society, but instead on the idea of black uplift founded on individual merit. This emphasis allowed Washington to break with the tradition of nineteenth-century black writing, the slave narrative. Rather than rely on Frederick Douglass for his inspiration, Washington looked to the popular figure of Abraham Lincoln—uneducated backwoods boy who became president, savior of the nation, emancipator of the race, and arguably the most legendary self-made man in post-Civil War America[18]—as his "patron saint" in literature (172). Elsewhere Washington judges that the abolitionist struggle "had not prepared Mr. Douglass [and other Negro leaders] to take up the equally difficult task of fitting the Negro for the opportunities and responsibilities of freedom."[19] Whereas Douglass demanded immediate and full citizenship for recently freed slaves, Washington lobbied for accommodationist proposals under which Americans of African descent were obliged to prove themselves worthy of full participation as citizens of the nation. Washington felt that the segregated economy provided the most pragmatic arena within which blacks could demonstrate the content of their character in the new century.

At the heart of *Up From Slavery* is Washington's famous 1895 Atlanta Exposition Address, which helped consolidate his hold on power in the eyes of Americans, white as well as black.[20] In the address he not only offered sensible advice to African Americans, particularly those living in the Black Belt, but lectured on the significance of self-help by pointing to the manner in which honest manual labor dignified the individual and the race. Furthermore, he maintained that blacks should "learn to draw the line between the superficial and the substantial, the ornamental gewgaws of life and the useful" (147). Earlier in the autobiography, Washington anticipates this anticonsumerist appeal with a tale about his own boyhood experience in the mining town of Malden, West Virginia. Upon entering school, young Booker felt pressure from his peers to acquire a store-bought cap. His mother decided otherwise, and displayed an impressive "strength of character" when she insisted that her son wear a homespun cap so that the family could continue to live within its means. Washington recalls retrospectively:

> I have noted the fact, but without satisfaction, I need not add, that several of the boys who began their careers with "store hats" and who were my schoolmates and used to join in the sport that was made of me because I had only a "homespun" cap, have ended their careers in the penitentiary, while others are not able now to buy any kind of hat. (46–47)

The anecdote is intended to illustrate the efficacy of the virtuous self and the hazards of wanton consumerism. Only character-based vigilance could keep conspicuous consumption from derailing one's efforts to climb the ladder of success.

Washington's Algeresque rags-to-respectability narrative is, like his promotion of industrial education for the black masses, an appeal to a residual Protestant ethos that valorized the development of inner morality. Echoing Carnegie's dictum, he insists that a black youth "gets a strength, a confidence, that one misses whose pathway is comparatively smooth by reason of birth and race." Echoing Du Bois, Washington claims that there is a peculiar benefit to membership in the "unpopular race," concluding that "often the Negro boy's birth . . .

is an advantage so far as real life is concerned." Yet, rather than developing the latter point into an argument for racially conscious enterprise, Washington immediately argues for merit-based black success. It is not race but "intrinsic, individual merit" (a "universal and eternal" law that applies equally to all Americans) that constitutes the basis for black enterprise (50).

Racial difference enters Washington's essentially color-blind narrative of self-making in circuitous ways. The moral luck of Alger's formula is, for instance, conspicuously absent from *Up From Slavery*. Moreover, the way this absence is staged suggests the extent to which luck is racially coded in conventional narratives of the self-made man. After completing his first year of study at Hampton Institute, Washington finds himself sixteen dollars in debt. Struggling to earn enough money with which to pay off his debt, he works in a restaurant during the summer recess. Still in debt a week before school re-opens, he finds "a crisp, new ten-dollar bill" under the table at his place of employment:

> I could hardly contain myself, I was so happy. As it was not my place of business I felt it to be the proper thing to show the money to the proprietor. This I did. He seemed as glad as I was, but he coolly explained to me that, as it was his place of business, he had a right to keep the money, and he proceeded to do so. This, I confess, was another pretty hard blow to me. (63)

Washington insists that he did not allow this piece of good-luck-turned-bad to become a source of discouragement. Thus, while offering his life story as an example of the efficacy of middle-class morality, the wizard of Tuskegee insists that his fame and fortune have nothing to do with luck, moral or otherwise. Later, he makes clear that "it was not luck" but "hard work" that ultimately brought him success (130). In his 1907 tract on the state of black enterprise in America, *The Negro in Business*, Washington extends this lesson to all members of the race: "I believe that the success won by hard work, rather than by lucky chance, is the only success that is of any importance to the race as a whole."[21]

Even if moral luck is absent from *Up From Slavery*, the author does not climb the ladder of success by pluck alone:

In those days, and later as a young man, I used to try to picture in my imagination the feelings and ambitions of a white boy with absolutely no limit placed upon his aspirations and activities. I used to envy the white boy who had no obstacles placed in the way of his becoming a Congressman, Governor, Bishop, or President by reason of the accident of his birth or race. I used to picture the way that I would begin at the bottom and keep rising until I reached the highest round of success. (50)

Washington is not being capricious, nor is he simply appropriating the most readily available model of uplift, which is racially coded. The boyhood obstacle described here is not encountered by Carnegie, whose assimilation into middle America takes the form of shedding a Scottish accent. Young Booker is obliged to imagine himself as white, a requirement shared by proponents of enterprise as diverse as Marcus Garvey and Younghill Kang.

Moral hygiene, rather than moral luck, is a cornerstone of black uplift in Washington's autobiography. For example, Mrs. Viola Ruffner, a white lady, demonstrates the efficacy of Christian virtue by providing him during his youth with an education in the art of cleanliness. In turn, he imparts this knowledge to his students. At Hampton Institute, Washington participates as a teacher in the "experiment" of educating Native Americans. He insists, contrary to the Indian's resistance to white customs, that not only the success but the survival of a race in industrial America depends on its ability to accommodate European culture: "but no white American ever thinks that any other race is wholly civilized until he wears the white man's clothes, eats the white man's food, speaks the white man's language, and professes the white man's religion" (81). Later, Washington extends these lessons in Western civilization to his students at Tuskegee Institute. Here, he puts into practice the middle-class ideals of "civilization, self-help, and self-reliance" (108) by making his students perform the domestic, agricultural, and industrial work related to the maintenance and growth of Tuskegee itself.

Tuskegee functions efficiently even in the absence of its president because its students' adherence to industrial time keeps the institutional gears well greased. Washington boasts that members of the college community are a "force . . . so organized and subdivided that the machinery of the school goes on day by day like clockwork" (170). The school is a civilizing machine that molds black students into industrial laborers under Jim Crow. Near the close of *Up From Slavery*, Washington provides evidence to support this claim: a complete "outline" of the student daily work schedule, from "5 A.M., rising bell" to "9.30 P.M., retiring bell" (201–2). The document, which resembles Franklin's famous "Scheme of Order," enforces the mechanisms of industrial time. Time at Tuskegee is oriented toward work and the refinement of behavior—hence, the Pavlovian "bells" that rouse the black student body. Washington introduces his outline for Tuskegee time in order to assure his audience that the student body is always "kept busy" and "out of mischief."

As Foucault explains, disciplinary time—deployed not only in schools, but also in prisons, hospitals, and factories—is "different than slavery because [it is] not based on a relation of appropriation of bodies." By controlling the operations of the body through the new microphysics of power, modern institutions "dispense with this costly and violent relation by obtaining effects of utility at least as great."[22] The adult Washington, as represented in *Up From Slavery*, bears these inscriptions of modern time. In the final passage in the book, just after he explains the logic behind the outline for daily work at Tuskegee, he quotes a flattering newspaper account of his own recent itinerary. The document details Washington's every move, including the times and places of each of his public appearances, and concludes that "the foremost educator among the colored people of the world" is "a very busy man" (203). It confirms that the head of Tuskegee practices what he preaches: the gospel of disciplined uplift.

Washington, however, did not care to recognize the extent to which black success was inhibited by its heightened subjection to the scrutiny of disciplinary institutions. *Up From Slavery* nonetheless stages the contradictions of modern time under Jim Crow. The most notable example is offered in the chapter "Boyhood Days," when young Booker confronts the first significant obstacle to self-made success in the form of reconciling his need to work in the West Virginia salt mines with his desire for an education. He confesses that, in order to work until nine o'clock in the morning and make it to school at the same time, he yielded to what was retrospectively an embarrassing temptation:

> There was a large clock in a little office in the furnace. This clock, of course, all the hundred or more workmen depended upon to regulate their hours of beginning and ending the day's work. I got the idea that the way for me to reach school on time was to move the clock hands from half-past eight up to the nine o'clock mark. This I found myself doing morning after morning, till the furnace "boss" discovered that something was wrong, and locked the clock in a case. I did not mean to inconvenience any body. I simply meant to reach that schoolhouse in time. (45–46)

Washington is not merely describing an indiscretion on the part of a poor but well-intentioned black youth. The institutional demands of the workplace and the schoolroom make it impossible for him to maintain a conventional relation to modern time. Carnegie, according to his *Autobiography*, was lifted off the factory floor and into a white-collar office only after jettisoning his unassimilated immigrant identity. I interpreted this recollection as an instance of racially coded moral luck, an element absent from *Up From Slavery*. Washington recollects that he had little choice but to distort industrial time so that he could be in two places at once. His boss soon discovered the boy's temporal transgression, reset the time, and placed a lock on the clock's case. The normative power of industrial order and moral discipline were thus restored.

Working Wonders: Madam C. J. Walker

Up From Slavery was published just a year after Booker T. Washington founded the influential National Negro Business League. The NNBL, bankrolled by his vocal supporter Andrew Carnegie, became the premier black entrepreneurial organization in the first half of this century.[23] Presiding over the thirteenth annual NNBL convention held in late August 1912 at the Institutional Church on Chicago's

South Side, Washington refused to interrupt the second day's schedule in order to yield the floor to a little-known, forty-four-year-old black woman named Madam C. J. Walker. On the third and final day, with outside temperatures hovering at 90 degrees, inside the convention hall even the sage of Tuskegee would not deny Madam Walker the chance to speak. Once again unable to gain recognition from Washington, she shouted from her seat in the audience: "Surely you are not going to shut the door in my face. I feel that I am in a business that is a credit to the womanhood of our race."[24]

In order to legitimate a female voice within the institutional apparatus of segregated enterprise, Madam Walker developed a unique if contradictory expression of African American women's agency. She appropriated and transformed the language of Horatio Alger uplift—according to the gospel of Booker T. Washington—in a manner that pointed to the moral efficacy of entrepreneurial endeavors for black womanhood. Walker thus opened her intervention at the 1912 NNBL convention by asserting that she was indeed "a credit to the womanhood of our race," and proceeded to testify to her remarkable, if not wholly unfamiliar, rags-to-riches story. She began: "I am a woman who started in business seven years ago with only $1.50."[25]

Walker, like pioneering cosmetics manufacturer Harriet Ayer before her, left only autobiographical fragments, forcing historians to reconstruct her life piecemeal from public statements made within specific institutional sites. She composed her life not in a room of her own but on the convention floor of Washington's National Negro Business League. Washington's imprint is visible on her August 1912 intervention into the male-dominated NNBL. Consider the way she concludes her speech from the convention floor:

> Now my object in life is not simply to make money for myself.... Perhaps many of you have heard of the real ambition of my life, the all-absorbing idea which I hope to accomplish, and when you have heard what it is, I hope you will catch the inspiration, grasp the opportunity to do something of far-reaching importance, and lend me your support. My ambition is to build an industrial school in Africa,—by the help of God and the cooperation of my

people in this country, I am going to build a Tuskegee Institute in Africa! (prolonged applause)[26]

By linking business success in segregated America to the uplift of Africa, Walker raises a story of individual self-making to the level of black nationalism. It is important to remember that her efforts on behalf of Africa were largely circumscribed by the Tuskegee machine. Today Washington is rarely remembered as a proponent of black nationalism. However, just after organizing the NNBL, he went into partnership with European investors in order to experiment with Tuskegee-style industrial education in Germany's African colonies.[27] This was black nationalism within what Wilson Moses terms its "civilizationist" tradition.[28]

Madam Walker's intervention before the 1912 NNBL convention stages the manner in which Du Bois's notion of "the advantage of the disadvantage" extended to a marketplace segregated not merely by the color line, but along gender lines as well. Before demonstrating further the monetary success of her "Wonderful Hair Grower" products by citing impressive increases in annual gross revenue over the previous six years, Walker interrupted her impromptu success story by stating: "I went into a business that is despised, that is criticized and talked about by everybody—the business of growing hair." Although male barbers might be revered within their community for the myriad tasks they performed, Walker's occupation was disparaged by a black middle class that was not only prone to gender and class bias but uneasy about the moral efficacy of indiscriminate consumerism. Specifically, the black bourgeoisie perceived hair dressing and straightening as menial work performed by lower-class black women; and hair growing was simply the province of con men.

Pausing before an NNBL audience now held captive by her audacious behavior, Walker coupled her frustration at gaining recognition on the convention floor with her prior attempts "to abandon the wash-tub for more pleasant and profitable occupation":

I have been trying to get before you business people and tell you what I am doing. I am a woman that came from the cotton fields of the South; I was promoted from there to the wash-tub (laughter); then I was promoted to the cook kitchen, and from there I promoted myself into the business of manufacturing hair goods and preparations.[29]

Walker's testimony is remarkable for its assertion of agency through black enterprise (from "I was promoted to . . ." to "I promoted myself . . ."). She suggests that her public identity was largely defined for her until she became self-employed and, hence, self-promotable. Nevertheless, by reading her story of self-promotion next to more conventional Progressive Era narratives of success, we begin to see the degree to which black patriarchy defined the meaning of female enterprise within segregated America.

Walker's gender-coded uplift story forced her audience to confront the plight of poor black women who had little choice but to accept menial domestic employment as laundresses, maids, and cooks.[30] Walker, attempting to seize the narrative authority of entrepreneurial self-making before an NNBL membership that was both awestruck and amused, pleaded: "Please don't applaud—just let me talk!" Walker's exclamation drew more laughter, but she pushed forward: "I am not ashamed of my past; I am not ashamed of my humble beginning. Don't think because you have to go down in the wash-tub that you are any less a lady!" (prolonged applause).[31] At stake for Walker was not just establishing her lowly start in life. She conveys to her audience that, despite the prevailing stereotype that labeled black women who labor in the fields or as domestics as unnaturally masculine, black womanhood is not sacrificed at the washtub. There is no shame, Walker insists, in work of any kind.

Madam Walker rose from being a sharecropper's daughter to becoming black America's most notable millionaire at a time when black businessmen were struggling to maintain a precarious foothold in the segregated marketplace. She had gone public with her rags-to-riches tale prior to her unannounced appearance before the NNBL convention in 1912. An extensive biographical sketch of her life was published in the 11 November 1911 edition of the *Indianapolis Freeman*, a nationally circulated black newspaper that just happened to have its base of operation in Madam Walker's recently adopted hometown.[32] This is the most complete contemporary account of her life on record. The newspaper biography reports Walker's birth, as Sarah Breedlove, to ex-slaves during the first days of Reconstruction. Her early years were spent on a Louisiana sharecropping farm. At seven, she was orphaned. Seven years later she wed a man named McWilliams; the *Freeman* puts it plainly: "She married at the age of fourteen in order to get a home."[33] A hard life in Vicksburg, Mississippi, was made more difficult when, at twenty, she was widowed and left to care for her only child. Walker and her daughter, like many African Americans living in the Black Belt during the post-Reconstruction era, left the South by following the Mississippi River north to Saint Louis. She found employment as a domestic in Saint Louis and, during this period, developed her miracle hair-treatment formula. She migrated west to Denver, Colorado, in order to make a business of her cosmetic discovery. In Denver she met and married her second husband, C. J. Walker, a black journalist who initially helped market her product. Despite the considerable potential for developing a profitable enterprise, the *Freeman* reports that C. J. Walker "discouraged" his wife from expanding her business because "he could see nothing ahead but failure."[34] Apparently ignoring the advice of her husband, she pursued her entrepreneurial ambition alone.

This early biographical sketch is notable for how it situates Walker's first husband as outside of and her second husband as an obstacle to her quest for success. When Madam Walker finally offered her story to a live audience—as she did every year at the NNBL (with one exception) between 1912 and 1916—she made only a passing mention of her widowhood and no reference at all to her second husband, whose initials and surname she made famous. The strained marriage ended in divorce. The absence of domestic life from Walker's uplift story (whether told by the *Freeman* or by herself) suggests the degree to which narratives of enterprise excluded married women, regardless of race, from autonomous public sphere success. Like Ayer, Walker was best equipped to make her mark in the business world when she was not wedded to the restricted expectations of a woman's role within the home. And, like Ayer, Walker's entrance into the marketplace was energized by, if restricted to, the emerging field of consumer-oriented manufacturing.

The *Annual Report* of the 1912 NNBL indicates that Washington was, at least publicly, unmoved by Walker's unscheduled address before his organization. Despite both the sensation her speech created on the floor and her nod to the important work of the wizard of Tuskegee, Washington apparently ignored Madam Walker by avoiding comment on her testimony and moving immediately to the next item of business on the agenda. This was no doubt due, in large part, to the fact that the NNBL (like all American entrepreneurial organizations of the time) was a men's club. Black women almost always attended these conventions as wives, if they attended at all.[35] Although Walker's ambition allowed her to elude many of the obstacles placed in front of her by the male-dominated NNBL, she never issued a systematic critique of the organization's expectations of black women.

The League's annual reports suggest that explicit criticism was not heard on the convention floor until 1917, when Mrs. D. Lampton Bacchus spoke unexpectedly (i.e., "at her request") on the topic "Woman—A Factor in Business." Elaborating on the type of obstacles confronting black female entrepreneurs, Lampton Bacchus states:

> Today she occupies a unique place in the world, being confronted by a woman question, a business and a race question, and yet, she is almost an unknown and an unacknowledged factor in each. We often find ourselves hampered with a very, very conservative attitude from those whose opinions we seek and respect most. This is not true of all our men, for had we not the support of them, no woman could succeed in business or be employed in the different occupations of men.[36]

Lampton Bacchus's own business experience—and her invitation to address the NNBL convention on this topic—was largely a result of family connections. Bishop E. W. Lampton of Greenville, Mississippi, had appointed his daughter to administer his considerable estate after his death. The means by which Lampton Bacchus entered the public sphere of business—that is, a family inheritance—was by far the most common avenue to entrepreneurship for women of any race. Moreover, her appeal on behalf of black womanhood should be placed within the legacy of African American women reformers that emerged at the end of the nineteenth century. This tradition included intellectuals and activists such as Frances Harper, Ida B. Wells, and Anna Julia Cooper. As Hazel Carby demonstrates, black women reformers in the late nineteenth and early twentieth centuries challenged the racist assumptions in conventional notions of femininity.[37] In doing so they articulated the unique predicament of black women, who were consistently denied access to the social authority and influence assigned to white women better able to fulfill the expectations prescribed by the cult of true womanhood.

Madam Walker, however, does not fit neatly into the tradition of black women intellectuals and activists. Although self-taught, she was not an intellectual; although a philanthropist, she cannot rightly be called a middle-class reformer. Nor can Walker, by the fact of her financial stake in the burgeoning personality industry, simply be assigned the role of disciple of Booker T. Washington. For these reasons, discussions of black uplift after the turn of the twentieth century are incomplete without accounting for Walker's conspicuous presence. Even by 1912, the year of her memorable if unexpected appearance before the National Negro Business League, the black press reported that she trained as sales agents nationwide "not less than 1,600 people, women mainly."[38] At the following year's NNBL convention, Walker made the slightly more modest claim of having given "employment to more than 1000 women." Nevertheless, she could boast that her agents "are now making all the way from $5, $10, and even as high as $15 a day."[39] These numbers are put into perspective when it is understood that, at this time, unskilled white workers earned under $2 per day and few black women made more than $1.50 *per week*.[40]

At the 1912 convention, Madam Walker forced open the door of the NNBL for black working-class women who labored in occupations considered less than respectable by the black bourgeoisie. The following year, Washington formally invited Walker to speak before the NNBL in Philadelphia on the practical subject of "Manufacturing Hair Preparations." She opened her first officially sanctioned address by announcing: "it would be more interesting and profitable for me to tell how I have succeeded in the business world, in order that other women of my race may take hold of similar work and make good." As a capitalist, Walker was primarily concerned with profits. As a self-promoter, she was interested in the art of the sale. She understood that the best way to sell her goods was to advertise herself through the language of virtuous uplift that was so familiar to her customers.

Yet Walker also viewed her own success as inextricably bound to uplifting her race. More specifically, she argued before the 1913 NNBL that her efforts to dignify the cosmetics industry would profit other black women too. Thus, prior to repeating the narrative of her triumphant plight from sharecropper to entrepreneur before the convention audience, she spoke of the unique obstacles facing black women in business. "The girls and women of our race must not be afraid to take hold of business endeavor and, by patient industry[,] close economy, determined effort, and close application to business, wring success out of a number of business opportunities that lie at their very doors."[41] Walker touted her own achievement in giving many women of her race the opportunity for employment as sales agents for her products. "I have made it possible," she concluded, "for many colored women to abandon the wash-tub for more pleasant and profitable occupation."[42] It was fast becoming a widely known fact that hundreds of black women were gainfully employed as Walker agents and, as such, instructed in the civic virtues of business success as well as cosmetics application.[43]

With Walker's 1913 NNBL address finished, Washington rose in order to direct the convention toward its next item of business. Yet, before doing so, he gave her a compliment, one that might be considered patronizing and even backhanded in view of the context in which it was uttered and the considerable laughter it drew from the floor: "You [fellow entrepreneurs] talk about what the men are doing in a business way, why if we don't watch out the women will excel us."[44] Indeed, Walker was excelling in every way. Her business was booming. Furthermore, as she toured the country giving lectures on the topic "The Negro Woman in Business," she was hailed in the black press as both black America's first millionaire and "America's

48

Foremost Colored Woman," who displayed a "philanthropic prominence classing with Helen Gould, John D. Rockefeller and Andrew Carnegie."[45]

The following year, Washington invited Walker—now considered the most famous entrepreneur in black America—to the NNBL's Fifteenth Annual Convention in Muskogee, Oklahoma. We might speculate that he learned a lesson from his prior encounter with her, for on this occasion he simply announced: "We are going to give [Madam Walker] five minutes' time in which she can talk about anything she chooses." Not surprisingly, Walker reiterated themes familiar to her audience—including references to her personal rags-to-riches story, to what she called "the struggle I am making to build up Negro womanhood," and to her philanthropic efforts at home and in Africa. In another audacious and thoroughly self-promoting gesture, she took the opportunity to request that the NNBL officially "endorse" her as the leading businesswoman in black America. Never one to play it safe, she concluded her 1914 address by seemingly returning the favor of Washington's compliment from the year before: "Everything that [Booker T. Washington] and his League are trying to do deserves and gets my warmest sympathy and support, and," she added, "if the truth be known there are many women who are responsible for the success of *you men*." When the laughter and applause ceased, the convention immediately gave Walker its endorsement as "the foremost business woman of our race."[46]

Walker's command over Washington's business league was now complete. Washington died prior to the following year's convention, which was devoted to eulogizing their fallen president and the Progressive Era's most prominent race leader. This makes Walker's apparent absence from the 1915 NNBL conference (her name never appears in the annual report) seem almost conspicuous. At the next year's 1916 annual meeting, she made a triumphant return to the League by declaring in her scheduled address: "I have now built up the biggest business owned and operated by Negroes anywhere in America."[47] No black entrepreneur, male or female, could challenge this boast. Soon thereafter Walker symbolically backed her colossal assertion by building on the Hudson River her Xanadu, a spectacular mansion dubbed Villa Lewaro by Enrico Caruso. Not just a spectacular mansion, Villa Lewaro was also a monument to conspicuous consumption and consumer desire in black America.

The evidence strongly suggests that, even prior to her outspoken debut at the 1912 NNBL gathering, Walker had mastered the conventional paradigm of the self-made man. Two and one-half years earlier she used her success story to advertise her makeover products in the local and national black media. On 16 April 1910, she publicly announced the new location of Walker Manufacturing Company by running her first advertisement in her hometown *Indianapolis Freeman*, one of the most widely read and respected black newspapers in the country. The ad for her Wonderful Hair Grower covered a full two-thirds of the newspaper's second page. About half of the space was covered with letters (eleven in all) from satisfied customers. One letter, for example, testified to the product's unequaled merits in "the art of growing hair." Walker also used her own likeness to promote her business. Atop the page for this ad was a "Before and After" photo of Madam Walker, a portrait that became a trademark when she put her face on the labels of her products. The text of the ad conveyed her eighteen years of frustration at losing her hair "until she made this wonderful discovery, which is now known to people throughout the country." Mainstream spokesmen for the gospel of American success had long promoted the partnership of God and Mammon. A shrewd saleswoman and self-described "Hair Culturist," Madam Walker was no stranger to this doctrine, which she exploited to gain the confidence of potential customers:

> During my many years of research, endeavoring to find something to improve my own hair, in preparations manufactured by others I was always unsuccessful, until through the Divine Providence of God I was permitted in a dream to discover the preparation that I am now placing at the disposal of the thousands who are today in the same condition that I was in, just three years ago.[48]

Not once, but at four separate moments in the Wonderful Hair Growing ad of April 1910, Walker explicitly credits God for bequeathing to her the magical hair care formula and for inspiring her to share it with others. Walker balanced the pitch for her product's ability to improve one's external appearance with the story of a divinely ordained discovery of the miracle hair grower. In this way, she created a hybrid form of self-made success, one that mixed moral luck and the new consumer desire for a magnetic personality.

The literature of success, as we have seen, typically codes luck as white. In appropriating the convention of divinely ordained uplift, Walker altered moral luck to meet the expectations of the black American consumer. For example, in an interview with the *Kansas City Star* (circa 1915), she repeated her story of entrepreneurial inspiration, but placed an African medium between herself and God— and suggested that the entire scenario appeared to her within a dream. "He answered my prayer, for one night I had a dream, and in that dream a big black man appeared to me and told me what to mix up for my hair. Some of the remedy was grown in Africa, but I sent for it, mixed it, [and] put it on my scalp."[49] The African continent, aside from transmitting inspiration to her entrepreneurial children across the sea, played a more tangible role in Walker's affairs. By 1914 she could claim before the NNBL annual convention that, among her other philanthropic endeavors, she was currently financing the education of five African children (three boys and two girls) at Tuskegee "for the purpose of founding and establishing a Negro Industrial School on the West Coast of Africa."[50]

Within a year before her own death in May 1919, Madam Walker's political and economic agenda for racial uplift at home and abroad took on a nationalist look that would soon be associated with Garveyism. She gladly offered her Hudson mansion as the site of at least one 1919 meeting of the International League of Darker Peoples (ILDP), a small group of activists whose members included A. Philip Randolph and Marcus Garvey. The ILDP, in rejecting President Wilson's proposal at Versailles that Europe continue to oversee Germany's African colonies, demanded that German Africa be replaced by a governing body composed of "enlightened sections" of the African diaspora.[51] Thus, while the demand for African self-rule marked a turn away from Booker Washington's limited partnership with European colonization, it nevertheless remained true to the "civilization-ist" legacy of American black nationalism.

On the home front, Walker, like many race leaders of her day, opposed social equality, a phrase associated with racial integration, while being a vocal supporter of the NAACP's antilynching cam-paign. "We don't want social equality with white folks," she was heard telling the delegates at the July 1918 Association of Colored Women convention in Denver. "We do want equality of opportunity" within black America.[52] It would be a mistake to read Walker's repudiation of social equality simply as a nod to black nationalism. Instead, it marks her intervention into the debate over black enterprise. Given that enterprising blacks faced the threat of lynching as well as busi-ness competition from white America, opposing racial integration while calling for equal opportunity made good business as well as po-litical sense. Decades after Madam Walker's death, when she was memorialized as a millionaire folk hero,[53] rumors circulated concern-ing the belief that her first husband, Moses McWilliams, was the vic-tim of a lynching. There is no factual evidence (of which I am aware) to support this claim. Yet, as A'Lelia Bundles suggests, the lynching of McWilliams is a "plausible fiction given the era."[54] Regardless, Walker's speech before the Association of Colored Women captured the considerable scope of her ambition. In the Age of Booker T. Washington, it displayed her business acumen; anticipating the com-ing of Jamaican-born immigrant Marcus Garvey, it manifested the politics of racial solidarity. Given the gathering of enterprising black women, it marked Madam Walker as a race woman of the first order.

4

Immigrant Aspirations

Out of America: Marcus Garvey

When twenty-nine-year-old West Indian Marcus Garvey reached the port of New York in March 1916, he stepped ashore and headed for Harlem where he roomed with a Jamaican family. He was not alone in his journey north. Harlem was the final destination for thousands of Caribbean immigrants who joined black Americans from the South in the Great Migration to the urban metropolis. Most newly arrived blacks had worked in rural settings and were now experiencing the unsettling process of proletarianization under an expanding industrial economy attempting to meet the demands of World War I.

The Back-to-Africa movement known as Garveyism captured the imagination of these recently displaced black agricultural workers. Its dynamic if potentially contradictory message wedded individual enterprise to racial solidarity in the service of building a black Palestine through mass migration to the African motherland. For an emerging black proletariat that dreamed of class mobility but whose opportunities were bound by segregation, Marcus Garvey offered a revision of Washington's famous but increasingly less relevant call to "cast down your buckets where you are." Speaking before his organization, the Universal Negro Improvement Association, in 1921, Garvey pointed out that the UNIA program

> seeks not to let the negro cast down his bucket where he is, but to have the bucket suspended and at the same time have a desire to build up himself as an independent force, as an independent factor in

the country that God Almighty gave him. . . . You cannot get away from the fact that the black man's—the colored man's—native habitat is Africa.[1]

Less than a year later, at the annual August UNIA convention, Garvey reconfirmed his organization's commitment to "the idea of fostering the industrial program set by Booker T. Washington, and in addition . . . the idea of nationhood—a government of our own so that our industries could be protected."[2] Garvey appropriated Washington's legacy of individual uplift and transformed it to meet the needs of the changing African American geopolitical terrain of around 1920.

Yet, unlike Washington, who attempted to transform Jim Crow into the self-made man by appealing to Christian morality, Marcus Garvey made positive racial difference grounded in national consciousness the basis of his appeal for black uplift. While Washington lectured that "the individual is the instrument, national virtue the end,"[3] Garvey revised this color-blind, character-based motto of American self-making by explicitly foregrounding race alongside nation: "As of the individual, so should it be of the race and nation."[4] Garvey, who resided in the United States between 1916 and 1927, believed that the African nation would open frontiers for the new Negro capable of uplifting the entire race. This argument tapped into the frustration of blacks who, on the whole, were less likely than other Americans to buy into the prevailing conception of individualism. Garvey seemed to understand the legacy of Tom Moss and other black businessmen in the United States who were lynched at the hands of angry if enterprising whites. "If you cannot get the same chance and opportunity alongside the white man," he stated at the height of his popularity in the United States in 1921, "then find a country of your own and rise to the highest position within that country."[5] Garvey offered black Americans entrepreneurial Pan-Africanism. Garveyism promoted a concept of African self-reliance that he first encountered while visiting Britain between 1912 and 1914, but that would become a product unique to the United States during the post–World War I era.

In his only sustained autobiographical composition, a 1923 essay titled "The Negro's Greatest Enemy," Garvey offers his life story as an example of the efficacy of wedding individual uplift to a positive racial identity. As a personal statement, the brief sketch provides few details that might assist the biographer.[6] I believe, however, that it is important to situate the self-composition within the context of what historian Robert Hill refers to as Garvey's "political retreat."[7] Garvey had been convicted on mail fraud charges, was incarcerated in New York City's Tombs Prison, and wrote "The Negro's Greatest Enemy" while awaiting the outcome of his appeal for bail. The boyhood portrait includes a tribute to his own father:

> I was born in the Island of Jamaica, British West Indies, on Aug. 17, 1887. My parents were black negroes. My father was a man of brilliant intellect and dashing courage. He was unafraid of consequences. He took human chances in the course of life, as most bold men do, and he failed at the close of his career. He once had a fortune; he died poor.[8]

The author not only comments on his father's capacity as a self-starter but uses the language of personality, fully in vogue after World War I, to describe the senior Garvey's captivating disposition.

Marcus Garvey situates his own awakening to racial consciousness within the context of Jamaica's two-tiered color-coded class/racial-caste hierarchy. Not until his "maturity" at age eighteen, he asserts, was racial prejudice a factor in his everyday life. He claims to have "got mixed up in public life" for the first time when, while a manager at a Kingston printing establishment, he "saw the injustice done to my race because it was black." The crisis in race relations compelled Garvey to leave Jamaica and travel throughout the West Indies, Central and South America, and finally Europe. He writes, repeatedly, "I found the same stumbling-block—'You are black.'"[9] Faced with racial obstacles to personal advancement prior to emigrating to the United States, Garvey groped for a means to understanding and improving his condition. According to the account given in "The Negro's Greatest Enemy," he stumbled onto a rosetta stone: "I read 'Up From Slavery,' by Booker T. Washington, and then my doom—if I may so call it—of being a race leader dawned upon me in London after I had traveled through almost half of Europe." He immediately asked himself: "'Where is the black man's Government?' 'Where is his King and his kingdom?' 'Where is his President, his country, and his ambassador, his army, his navy, his men of big affairs?' I could not find them, and then I declared, 'I will help to make them.'"[10] Placing Booker T. Washington at the center of his personal statement not only made Garvey's life more readable to U.S. audiences. It also gave him a way of making black nationalism relevant to the lives of a recently uprooted black working class.

Early in 1915, the twenty-seven-year-old Garvey wrote Booker T. Washington telling him of his plans for a Tuskegee-style industrial school in Jamaica and asking for his support. When he wrote again, stating his intention to visit the United States, the foremost black American leader responded politely, offering to make the young Jamaican's stay "as pleasant and as profitable as we can."[11] As Washington's biographer suggests, it is likely that he misinterpreted Garvey's intentions, believing UNIA to be a flattering imitation of his own National Negro Business League.[12] Washington died only months after his correspondence with Garvey, but his influence on the latter did not diminish with his passing.

Tuskegee provided an inspirational, if not actual,[13] blueprint for the UNIA and its most ambitious entrepreneurial project, a steamship company named the Black Star Line (BSL). From the moment of his 1916 arrival on the mainland to his federal deportation in 1927, Garvey linked individual enterprise to black nationalism. In doing so, he laid claim to Washington's legacy as the foremost race leader in the United States. In the mid-twenties, when the efficacy of the UNIA and its uplift projects was in doubt due to public scrutiny, government infiltration, and internal mismanagement, black newspapers continued to measure Garvey's achievements alongside the accomplishments of Washington. In 1924, after the irrepressible Jamaican purchased the fourth vessel (the *General G. W. Goethals*) of the BSL fleet and announced his plan to rechristen it the *Booker T. Washington*, he drew a mixed reaction. In the September issue of the *Chicago Defender*, a journalist frequently critical of Garvey did not miss the opportunity to comment: "No one objects to Mr. Garvey owning ships or going back to Africa. American colored people do object to his taking the name of their greatest man as a title to his comedy. The name of his vessel ought to be the 'Marcus A. Garvey.' Booker T. Washington was a SUCCESS."[14] At the same moment, the *Harlem News* editorialized that, despite Garvey's blunders, the leader of the UNIA had "awakened the race consciousness and race pride of the masses of Africans everywhere as no man ever did . . . save Booker T. Washington."[15] The historical misreading in this statement reveals the influence that Garvey had on black America of the period. Only in the wake of Garvey, who persistently attempted to ally himself with the sage of Tuskegee, could Washington's efforts be remembered as an attempt to stimulate "the race consciousness and race pride" in the African diaspora. Nevertheless, the organic appeal of Garvey's message was based on an ideal promoted by Booker Washington and the National Negro Business League: namely, blacks should invest their money in black-owned businesses. The Negro Moses put it this way: "The Black Star Line corporation presents to every Black Man, Woman and Child the opportunity to climb the great ladder of industrial and commercial progress. . . . The [BSL] will turn over large profits and dividends to stockholders, and operate to their interest even whilst they will be asleep."[16]

For Garvey, black enterprise was the motor of individual opportunity and the progress of the race. As Edmund David Cronon points out, financial speculation in the UNIA's Black Star Line or in its Negro Factory Corporation allowed blacks to claim for themselves a success previously associated only with white financiers, such as the Wall Street wizard J. Pierpont Morgan.[17]

Garvey readily acknowledged the significance of Washington's *Up From Slavery* on his own emergence as the most popular race leader in America during the 1920s.[18] As we saw earlier, the broad-based appeal of *Up From Slavery* was due, in large part, to its author's ability to appropriate for black men the rhetorical conventions of Anglo-Saxon entrepreneurial success without explicitly challenging racist institutions and practices. While in the United States, Garvey also spoke within the individualistic language of the American Way.

In a 1919 Philadelphia speech, he preached "self-reliance wherein the Negro must do for himself,"[19] and, in 1921, he told a journalist that "no man will do as much for you as you will do for yourself."[20] Garvey's writing on uplift also displayed the masculinist inflection common to nationalist narratives of self-making, black or white. In a 1922 editorial published in the UNIA's organ, *Negro World*, he states: "The first thing th[at] we will have to do is to remake ourselves, lift ourselves from the conditions of slavery, of being lackeys, parasites or wards, to the position of real men, men of initiative, men of brawn and power, men of great accomplishments."[21] Although Garvey might praise the entrepreneurial achievements of Madam Walker,[22] his speeches and writings suggest that he believed that "real men" remade themselves in steel and shipping trades rather than by manufacturing hair-care products or perfume. In turn, he advised the women of his race to conform to racially coded middle-class standards of true womanhood: "be true to your men," he told black women, "be as true to your men in this crisis as the white women have been to their men through all their difficulties."[23]

Although Garvey was a black leader in the nineteenth-century "civilizationist" tradition, he also spoke directly to a newly awakened black diaspora by celebrating the common history and inherent racial uniqueness of Africans at home and throughout the world. Nonetheless, from at least the time of his first trip to Britain in 1912, Garvey believed that, without an Anglicized culture, members of the African diaspora lacked the means for racial uplift and were destined for extinction. Upon his return to Jamaica two years later, he immediately gained a brash reputation among the black and colored Jamaican elite. He scolded them for their "callous indifference and insincerity" toward the vast majority of the population, who were black, poor, and "still ignorant and backward." More directly, they had "failed to do their duty by the race in promoting a civilized imperialism that would meet with the approval of established ideals."[24] Soon afterward, he settled on the idea that the black man required "a nation and a country of his own, where he can best show evidence of his own ability in the art of human progress."[25]

In a well-publicized address delivered in Kingston six months before his arrival in the United States, Garvey continued to indict the "cultured class" that would rather avoid than confront the "uncouth and vulgar" environs of the Jamaican masses.[26] Alternatively, the Universal Negro Improvement Association, which Garvey headed, "has set itself the task to go among the people and help them up to A BETTER STATE OF APPRECIATION among the cultured classes, and raise them to the standard of civil[iz]ed approval." Booker T. Washington cast a long shadow over Garvey's speech: he is mentioned at the beginning, middle, and end of the address. The 1914 speech made explicit the degree to which Washington's authorizing signature was written upon Garvey's maturing public persona. The address, which was reprinted in the *Jamaican Daily Chronicle*, incited a heated debate. One vocal opponent of Garvey at the time, a colored Jamaican professional named Leo S. Pink, attempted to use the Washington mystique to deflate the posturing of the young UNIA president: "Booker T. Washington worked earnestly for his race and is entitled to the position he now occupies, and Mr. Garvey must not think for one moment he can be a Booker Washington, as great men are born, not made."[27] Pink apparently had not read *Up From Slavery*. The president of the UNIA, on the other hand, was already well versed in tales of American success prior to his arrival in the United States.

At this time, as Judith Stein observes, there was a general agreement among leaders, black and white, that the model of "European . . . planning and efficiency" could provide the means for bringing Africa into the modern world.[28] Garvey's popularity can be attributed to his ability to wed the imperialist example of white industrialists and financiers to a message of Pan-African pride. The UNIA's Black Star Line was the perfect vehicle for imagining, if not fulfilling, his Back-to-Africa program. In the wake of World War I, commercial shipping became increasingly important to the U.S. strategy of dominance in global affairs. Not only was the American navy the focus of its war efforts but, as Stein elaborates, after the armistice the new American fleet became the means by which the United States could sustain and expand its overseas markets.[29] Garvey's grand schemes were financed, in part, by the relative affluence of black Americans, who indirectly benefited from the economic prosperity of the United States on the world market during the post-war period. In an effort to raise sufficient capital to purchase steam-ships for the BSL fleet, the UNIA sold stock shares to its black con-stituency, who resided primarily in the United States and, to a lesser extent, in the Caribbean.[30] "If we are to rise as a great [people] to be-come a great national force, we must start business enterprises of our own," stated Garvey in 1919. More specifically, "we must build ships and start trading with ourselves between America, the West Indies and Africa."[31] The Black Star Line reversed the direction of the At-lantic slave trade, transforming the infamous Middle Passage into a Pan-Africanist shipping as well as emigration route for "the purpose of bettering the industrial and economic condition of the race."[32]

Garvey found himself in the contradictory position of promot-ing the activities of corporate captains of industry while criticizing their imperialist interests abroad. He made one of his earliest public references to Anglo-Saxon self-made men on the final day of the 1922 UNIA convention. In the process of asking Americans of African de-scent to redirect their savings and investments from white-controlled Wall Street institutions to the black-owned UNIA organizations, Garvey offered ideas on the white way to wealth:

> God never made rich men. How did men come to be rich? By being able to fool the other folks. If you read the lives of million-aires like Carnegie and Rockefeller you will find that they never started with anything. They were not born rich, they got rich by working out plans by which they would get people to work for them. . . . All that he uses is brains to harness your labor and the whole country of white people is working for these few men of brains who sit down in Wall Street.[33]

Garvey, apparently an avid reader of entrepreneurial autobiographies, believed that millionaires were not born but made by the power of their minds. His appeal to mind power as a means to business em-pire—which, Robert Hill points out, had its most significant impact on the leader of the UNIA only after he was deported from the United States[34]—was indebted to the spread of the New Thought philosophy of success in the first few decades of this century.

Regardless, the imperialist-based schemes of the Rockefellers, the

Firestones, and the Carnegies—which amassed fortunes for American captains of industry in the name of civilized human progress for underdeveloped nations—posed a problem for Garvey. What was the difference between the overseas entrepreneurial adventures of these white men and his own blueprint for establishing black-owned corporations in the motherland? As early as April 1923, Garvey began pointing out that when white capitalists look toward the dark continent, it is not with the interests of Africans in mind: "The white man is now" developing Africa "not with the intention of building for other races, but with the intention of building for himself—for the white race."[35]

> If the oil of Africa is good for Rockefeller's interest; if iron ore is good for the Carnegie Trust; then surely these minerals are good for us. Why should we allow Wall Street and the capitalist group of America and other countries to exploit our country when they refuse to give us a fair chance in the countries of our adoption? Why should not Africa give to the world its black Rockefeller, Rothschild and Henry Ford?[36]

According to the logic of Garvey's words, imperialism in Africa is a problem when white captains of industry exploit the raw materials of the continent; it is a virtue when it grants the opportunity to bring forth entrepreneurs from the black diaspora. As he saw it, the task at hand was for blacks worldwide "to make a desperate effort to reconquer our Motherland," and protect her from the "selfish exploitation and domination" of white men. With a fervor reminiscent of nineteenth-century Christian missionaries, he writes: "If native Africans are unable to appreciate the value of their own country from the standard of Western civilization, then it is for us, their brothers, to take to them the knowledge and information that they need to help to develop the country."[37]

Black Americans, unlike Jamaicans and other West Indians, were not living under a colonial doctrine according to which England or France was the mother country. Garvey recognized this difference, and cultivated among blacks in the United States a collective racial consciousness that confirmed Africa as their national origin. The United States, in turn, might be seen as a port of departure for black

Americans who desired to emigrate to Africa. Yet, aside from his personal entanglements with the law, two problems overwhelmed Garvey's dream of what he once called the "United States of Africa."[38] First, moving millions of people across the Atlantic involved an array of nearly insurmountable practical hurdles. Second, by the 1920s native-born blacks increasingly thought of themselves as U.S. citizens first and African descendants second. This must have been difficult for a West Indian emigrant to comprehend. For Garvey, who insisted, "I was born in an alien country [Jamaica],"[39] America was a long way from the promised land. The United States functioned, instead, as his inspirational and practical port of departure.

From Steerage to Self-Culture: Mary Antin

For most immigrants who came to the United States during the late nineteenth and early twentieth centuries, America became a final resting place if not a paradise of riches. The Progressive Era not only witnessed the largest wave of immigration to the nation's shores, but also saw the composition of the foreign-born population shift from northwestern to southeastern Europeans.[40] The great wave, lasting roughly from 1890 to 1920, coincided with a period in U.S. history when the idea of the self-made man was at its most popular. How did the idea of American success influence the lives of new arrivals, particularly those who, although not black, emigrated from countries outside northwestern Europe? What impact, if any, did the visibility of these strangers in America have on the figure of the self-made man in the new century? Traditionally, the heroes of uplift stories were not only white and male but northern European too. After the Civil War, as long as newcomers continued to migrate mainly from Germany and Britain, native-born Americans had little reason to feel that their cultural traditions were threatened by outsiders. As John Higham points out, even nativists of the 1880s were confident that the Anglo-Saxon had "a marvelous capacity for assimilating kindred races, absorbing their valuable qualities, yet remaining basically unchanged."[41]

The venerated Gilded Age self-made man, Scottish immigrant Andrew Carnegie, concurred with this assessment. He agreed that

America was a melting pot, but of a very narrow kind. New arrivals would ideally be assimilated as Anglo-Americans. In the opening sentence of a chapter titled "The American People" from his *Triumphant Democracy* (1886), the steel magnate professed his faith that newcomers could be absorbed into the national culture of the United States. "Fortunately for the American people," he stated, "they are essentially British."[42] In the year that Carnegie published *Triumphant Democracy*, only 16 percent of all immigrants to the United States originated in the eastern and southern regions of the Old World. Ten years later, in 1896, new immigrants from southeastern Europe stock outnumbered "old immigrants" for the first time. By the middle of the next decade, 75 percent of all new arrivals came from eastern and southern Europe, and the largest portion of these were Russian Jews and southern Italians. New immigrants were distinguishable from the old in a number of ways: they practiced a religion other than Protestantism, they resided in the crowded urban ghettoes, and they became industrial wage earners rather than agricultural workers. Many native-born citizens perceived them to be a class apart inasmuch as they seemed less assimilable and more impoverished than earlier arrivals.

After the turn of the century, according to Higham, the increase in new immigrants coincided with the rise of a new type of nativism based on racial, rather than primarily religious, prejudice. In the first decade of the twentieth century, nativists began to exploit the language of white Anglo-Saxon superiority.[43] The earliest and most significant manifestation of the new nativism came in 1906 when Congress attempted to enact a literacy test in order to curtail emigration from southeastern Europe. Although the literacy test was defeated, Congress established the U.S. Immigration Commission (aka the Dillingham Commission) to study the problem. The federal agency was charged with investigating "the changed character of the immigration movement to the United States over the past twenty-five years." As such, the commission started with the following presupposition: "The old and the new immigration differ in many essentials." Whereas the old immigrant arrived from the "most progressive sections of Europe for the purpose of making for themselves homes in the New World," the new immigrant was characterized as "unskilled laboring men who have come, in large part temporarily, from the less progressive and advanced countries of Europe." Assimilation for new immigrants, it was believed, "has been slow as compared to that of the earlier non-English-speaking races."[44]

Behind the Dillingham study was the increasingly commonplace assumption that the new immigrants were an inferior breed, and thus less qualified than their European forerunners to be Americans. It was against a mounting tide of nativism that Mary Antin published her tract *They Who Knock at Our Gates* (1914). A first-generation Russian Jew, she defended new immigrants by imagining a continuum between old-stock Americans and recent arrivals. "The ghost of the Mayflower pilots every immigrant ship," chanted Antin, "and Ellis Island is another name for Plymouth Rock."[45] In the opening pages, she acknowledges: "Granted that Sicilians are not Scotchmen, how does that affect the right of a Sicilian to travel in pursuit of happiness?" For Antin, America was symbolized by what her friend, playwright Israel Zangwill, had recently dubbed "the melting pot"—a place where distinctions along lines of descent were softened, where an Italian Catholic had the same opportunity to climb the ladder of success as Andrew Carnegie.[46] In *They Who Knock at Our Gates*, Antin looks into the face of the new immigrant and envisions "a self-made man":

> There is a phrase in the American vocabulary of approval that sums up our national ideal of manhood. That phrase is "a self-made man." To such we pay the tribute of our highest admiration, justly regarding our self-made men as the noblest product of our democratic institutions. Now let any one compile a biographical dictionary of our self-made men, from the romantic age of our history down to the prosaic year of 1914, and see how the smell of the steerage pervades the volume![47]

Antin's polemical prose enacts a counternarrative as she transforms the rags-to-riches Christian into the pungent self-made immigrant.

Prior to the appearance of *They Who Knock at Our Gates*, Antin had adroitly appropriated the language of American self-making in order to introduce herself to a largely Protestant readership. *The Prom-*

ised Land, Antin's widely read immigrant autobiography of 1912, opens
with the pronouncement: "I was born, I have lived, and I have been
made over. . . . I am absolutely other than the person whose story I
have to tell."[48] The enthusiastic reviews of *The Promised Land*, coupled with its impressive sales, suggest the effectiveness of her rhetorical strategy.[49] The book's success can be partly attributed to the fact
that it falls within a uniquely American heritage of self-composition
dating back to Franklin. Unlike the most prominent Jewish immigrant writer of her era, Abraham Cahan, Antin does not dwell on the
abiding sense of religious and cultural alienation suffered by over-
achieving immigrants. And, unlike Korean writer Younghill Kang,
who was subjected to the explicitly racist forms of nativism during
the Tribal Twenties, Antin's Progressive Era autobiography demonstrates the efficacy of the melting-pot model of success.

It is symptomatic of Antin's adherence to the melting-pot paradigm in *The Promised Land* that she is unable to see how African
Americans might be at a disadvantage even in their encounter with
new arrivals. In a brief but telling childhood recollection, Antin describes how a neighborhood black boy, whom she accuses of bullying
her, is taken to court by her father and punished with imprisonment.
"[T]he moral of this incident," the author remarks, "was what I saw
of the way in which justice was actually administered in the United
States. Here we were gathered in the little courtroom, bearded Arlington Street against wool-headed Arlington Street. . . . We were all
free, and all treated equally, just as it said in the Constitution!" (260).
Antin's blindness to the racial coding of morality if not justice should
not be understood as a personal oversight that lies outside Progres-
sivism. Racism lies within the logic of a movement that routinely saw
nothing disingenuous in the "separate but equal" axiom of Jim Crow.
However, in what is otherwise an optimistic immigrant narrative of
New World promises fulfilled, Antin's frustration with her entrepreneurial ambitions is overdetermined by her unequal footing in the
male-dominated marketplace as a woman.

The key to immigrant uplift and assimilation in America is, for
Antin, the nation's fledgling public school system. "The public school
has done its best for us foreigners," she asserts in *The Promised Land*,

adding "and for the country, when it has made us into good Americans" (222). The author goes to great lengths to demonstrate how American schools manifest the ideals of self-made success by promoting freedom of opportunity. Antin claims that, while attending Boston public schools immediately after her arrival in 1894, her education in U.S. history forced her to "revise" her self-estimation. Here she is exposed to the patriotic theme "Fellow Citizens"—and, more specifically, to America's First Fellow Citizen, George Washington. Not only is the eager student in awe of such an inimitable historical figure, but, she reflects, "the twin of my new-born humility, paradoxical as it may seem, was a sense of dignity I had never known before. For if I found that I was a person of small consequence, I discovered at the same time that I was more nobly related than I had ever supposed" (224). Star-spangled statements such as this have caused commentators, at least since the 1930s, to cast a skeptical eye across the pages of *The Promised Land*. The book has been criticized for its naive celebration of the American Way, especially when compared to the realist portraits of ambitious immigrants created in the fiction of Cahan.[50]

The standard reproach to Antin's optimistic autobiography can be maintained only when the critic overlooks how femininity functions in the book to work against the grain of a celebratory story of immigrant uplift. Only when the gendered contradictions of Antin's immigrant self-making are taken into account do the economic hardships she and her family suffered come into sharp focus. Throughout *The Promised Land*, the women in Antin's family constitute the antithesis of the ideals embodied by the self-made man. Her mother, at times the primary breadwinner in the Old World, is repeatedly characterized as "self-effacing" in the New (246). Her older sister, Frieda, fairs little better as her "path of duty" leads only to a domestic dead end (252) and, after the family's arrival in Boston, to the factory floor of a garment shop (277). Alternatively, Mary is able to take advantage of opportunities for personal uplift not only because she has pluck but also because she is endowed with good fortune: "I differed from [Frieda] a little in age, considerably in health, and enormously in luck" (99). This, however, does not explain Mary's younger sister, Dora. Although she has all the advantages afforded Mary, Dora gravitates, like Frieda, toward traditional women's roles.[51] As for herself, the author simply states: "I did not like housework" (255).

Young Mary, like Alger's fictional Tattered Tom, is able to imagine herself as an enterprising individual so long as she is misrecognized as a boy. Throughout the autobiography, Antin expresses her youthful desire "to play the tomboy" (259, 266, 335), an identity that affords her entry into the public arena of the self-made man. Her adolescent reading list duplicates the masculine success literature found on the childhood shelves of ambitious women such as Ida B. Wells. Second only to stories written by Louisa Alcott, claims Antin, "were boys' books of adventure, many of them by Horatio Alger; and I read all, I suppose, of the Rollo books, by Jacob Abbott" (257):

> In the boys' books I was fond of reading I came across all sorts of heroes, and I sympathized with them all. The boy who ran away to sea; the boy who delighted in the society of ranchmen and cowboys; the stage-struck boy, whose ambition was to drive a pasteboard chariot in a circus; the boy who gave up his holidays in order to earn money for books; the bad boy who played tricks on people; the clever boy who invented amusing toys for his blind little sister—all these boys I admired. I could put myself in the place of any one of these heroes, and delight in their delights. (322)

Poor Frieda, the author laments, "had little enough time for reading, unless she stole it from the sewing or the baking or the mending." The four walls of that kitchen "bounded her life" (337–38). Alternatively, sister Mary describes herself as the "imaginative growing child" (190).

In a provocative chapter titled "The Landlady," Antin stages the gender restrictions placed on an immigrant girl. The reader learns that her family's inability to keep up with the weekly rent for their Dover Street apartment was a persistent source of anxiety for their seventeen-year-old daughter. Being "particularly ambitious to earn the rent," Mary finds a job soliciting subscriptions for a local paper (301). Possessing all of the optimistic energy of an Alger street urchin, Antin encounters only men in the downtown Boston business district and sells only one subscription. A potential patron advises her that "he did not think it was a nice business for a girl, going through the offices like that. This took me aback. I had not thought anything about the nature of the business. I only wanted the money to pay the rent. I wandered through miles of stone corridors, unable to see why it was not a nice business, and yet reluctant to go on with it, with the doubt in my mind" (306). Before Antin figures out why soliciting subscriptions is inappropriate for young women, another potential customer adds insult to injury by misidentifying her as a common beggar rather than the enterprising youth she intends herself to be. Although the author simply describes her loss of faith in the product she peddles (308), the careful reader can not help but recognize the limits placed on entrepreneurial success for a woman.

Tired, hungry, and feeling uncharacteristic self-pity as a result of her business failure, Antin drifts into fantasy. She imagines herself lost and destitute on the rough streets of Boston. Without hope, she faints on a stranger's doorstep and is found dead the next morning. An optimistic fantasy, however, quickly replaces the nightmare: "I might faint at the door of a rich old man's house, who would take me in, and order his housekeeper to nurse me, just like in the story books" (308). The poor but virtuous girl falls into favor with a wealthy gentleman, who takes her home to Dover Street ("in a carriage!") where she is happily reunited with her family. He offers her father gainful employment, which allows the family to move out of their ghetto apartment and into a pastoral home ("with a garden around it"). Antin returns from escapist dreams to a bleak and humiliating reality. In a state of desperation over the rent, she makes the mistake of attempting to reason with her landlady, Mrs. Hutch. Antin explains to Mrs. Hutch that she intends "to go to college, to fit myself to write poetry, and get rich, and pay the arrears." The landlady abruptly cuts her off by scoffing at the idea of "lazy" immigrant "beggars" going to college: "You ought to go to work, if you know enough to do one sensible thing." The enterprising girl was at an impasse. "I tried to sell papers, for the sake of the rent," she recollects as she flees her landlady's home in shame, "and I was told it was not a nice business" (315–17).

Despite the buoyant mood of *The Promised Land*, Antin is ultimately unable to cast her own success in terms of the narrative of the self-made man. If she is unwilling to be explicitly critical of America for thwarting her aspirations, Antin's autobiography nevertheless performs this operation by what is left unsaid in its conclusion. Here, she addresses an anticipated question from her readership regarding the financial rewards presumed to accompany her achievements. "Did I get rich? you may want to know, remembering my ambition to provide for the family." She replies: "I have earned enough to pay Mrs. Hutch the arrears, and satisfy all my wants. And where have I lived since I left the slums? My favorite abode is a tent in the wilderness" (360). If the promised land does not pay off for Antin, she finds refuge in nature. This explains why she concludes her autobiography by recounting an anecdote about her emergence as a "practicing naturalist" (363).

Antin maintains that she discovered "the genuine, practical equality" missing from other areas of her life in the Hale House Natural History Club. It was her club membership—and not her entrepreneurial endeavors—"which played an important part in my final emancipation from the slums" (362). The author describes an excursion to study marine life, where she is exposed to nature's mysteries. It is an experience full of wonderment for Antin, which ultimately allows her to forge a deeply felt connection between herself and the promised land. "The tide had rushed in at its proper time, stealing away our seaweed cushions, drowning our transparent pools, spouting in the crevices, booming and hissing, and tossing high the snowy foam. . . . The members of the club . . . discussed the day's successes, compared specimens, exchanged field notes, or watched the western horizon in sympathetic silence" (363). Antin, a student of nineteenth-century Transcendentalist philosophy, locates her own narrative of uplift in the Emersonian idea of higher laws and, more specifically, in Thoreau's experience at Walden Pond. Emerson's conception of the Oversoul, which expresses the unity of self and nature, provides her with an alternative to commercialism.[52] Only in this way does Antin vindicate her faith in the United States as the land of what Emerson called the "self-helping man"—the exemplar of self-culture who strives to nourish his hungry soul rather than stockpile his bank account.[53]

Oriental Yankees: Younghill Kang

Chungpa Han—the autobiographical narrator of Younghill Kang's *East Goes West: The Making of an Oriental Yankee*[54]—echoes the spirit of Mary Antin's immigrant narrative when, upon arriving in America in 1922, he states: "I entered a new life like one born again."[55] Born in a northern province of Korea in 1903, Kang lived through the humiliating first decade of Japanese occupation. Kang resided in Seoul during the tumultuous year of 1919, where he found himself translating *Pilgrim's Progress* for a Western missionary while protesting Japanese colonial rule by participating in the March First (Sam Il) independence movement. Disillusioned by Korea's inability to respond effectively to colonial occupation, he developed the unshakable desire "to escape death and torture if possible and to come to America."[56] He arrived in New York City at the age of eighteen, just three years prior to a statute mandating the end of Korean immigration and completing a long-standing policy of Asian exclusion. While Kang struggled economically and emotionally as a "foreign student," he kept his distance from the Korean independence movement in America. He put his energies into finding employment that would, aside from allowing him to complete degrees in prestigious U.S. universities, open doors toward fulfilling his desire to remake himself through entrepreneurial success.

Historian Oscar Handlin judges that the harsh reality of immigrant existence was "not congenial to the ideal of the self-made businessman."[57] Kang's autobiographical novel suggests the extent to which, for a Korean in the 1920s, the lack of congeniality in the arena of enterprise was rooted in nativism and racial prejudice. Chungpa Han's "first American step . . . in economic life" (57), for example, is as a cook's helper in an upper-class white home. Here he is immediately exposed to racial hierarchies within the United States. His employer informs him that he and a Korean friend are replacing a hardworking Negro cook because she believes they will be more "presentable" than a black servant (63). Within a week, however, Han is fired for ineptitude. This is the first in a series of instances in which the Korean immigrant's lack of familiarity with Western business practices coupled with the nativist attitudes of his employers results in his failure to get a foot onto the ladder of marketplace achievement.

Contemporary reviewers of *East Goes West* interpreted the book as an optimistic celebration of the immigrant in America, perhaps akin to Antin's *Promised Land*. More recently, Elaine Kim has responded to these misreadings by flatly stating that Kang's book "is not a minority success story."[58] Indeed, the fictional autobiography not only represents Han as a failed entrepreneur but illustrates the difficult, often racist, conditions under which Koreans labored in America. It is important to add, however, that Kang's work demonstrates the *productivity* of failed immigrant uplift in the 1920s. More specifically, the author appropriates the language of self-made success not simply to illustrate his victimization in the New World but also as a means of representing the process by which a Korean's ethnic identity is fashioned and refashioned even under the most restrictive forms of nativism.

In Kang's first autobiographical novel, *The Grass Roof*, the author examines the differences between East and West primarily through the concept of individual enterprise. The narrator, Han, describes his Buddhist upbringing within a Korean society where a precapitalist mode of accumulation endured and where the idea of the "individual" or "success" remained foreign. Until recently, he informs us, Korea and other Asian cultures devalued business enterprise relative to other worldly pursuits: "According to Korean, Chinese, and Japanese social system of the old days, business almost was the lowest occupation, the order being scholars, agriculturists, artisans and merchants, coolies and dog-slayers."[59] Alternatively, the figure of the self-made man provides the immigrant Han with a newly conceived identity. As he prepares for his Occidental voyage at the conclusion of *The Grass Roof*, Han rationalizes the prohibitive cost by casting himself in the same mold as an American original: "After paying my passage I was almost penniless, like young Benjamin Franklin arriving in Philadelphia."[60] Nearly two hundred years to the day after Franklin disembarked from the Market Street Wharf in Philadelphia, Kang's autobiographical narrator steps off a steamship in the New York harbor with four dollars in his pocket. At the opening of *East*

Goes West, Han wanders the city streets aimlessly and, by the afternoon of his second day, is left with a dime. Despite such hardships, he remains optimistic: "My first American step," he tells his Americanized Korean friend named George, "I will make money" (57). Yet, as an Asian immigrant, Han makes more of an awkward appearance than Franklin ever imagined for himself. He attempts to improve his look with a visit to the barbershop, although his first job interview proves a failure when he learns that the prospective employer is not hiring Negroes or Orientals.

In the most immediate sense, Han's business ventures are a means to fulfilling the promise of a Western education offered by "the land of golden opportunity" (134). Yet, in repeated efforts to fulfill his New World expectations, Han finds less than ideal employment in the area of retail sales—both on the road (peddling encyclopedias) and on the floor of a major department store (where his identity as an Oriental is exploited in the service of selling chinaware). The lessons Han learns in business become the foundation for his education not just in American consumerism but in the forms that racism and nativism take in the United States. His most extensive exposure to the art of the sale comes in the form of an encounter with Mr. D. J. Lively, the bullish owner of the Universal Education Publishing Company. Lively, whose tautological motto is "The successful salesman *is* a success" (154), suggests putting Han to work selling the *Universal Education* encyclopedia. When his prospective employee explains how "very hard" it is "for an Oriental to learn American salesmanship," he gives Han the hard sell on the "spirit of American optimism."

Kang's representation of Lively appears as a gloss on the teachings of Bruce Barton, who during the 1920s popularized the life of Jesus Christ by envisioning him as an enterprising prophet with a magnetic personality.[61] More specifically, Lively promotes retail sales to Han with an inspiring account of how the nation's founding father, George Washington, got his start as a drummer:

> "How I do like to see manly independence! The spirit that inspired Abraham Lincoln and George Washington. The spirit back of these United States of America. Nothing is too small by which to make honest money. George Washington, the father of his coun-

try, was only a poor bookseller once. Did you know that, my boy? Yes, a poor bookseller." He made an impressive pause. "And the man you see before you, too. D. J. Lively. That's how he got his start. The selling business." (142–43)

Successful sales skills are, Lively suggests, essential to nation building. He recognizes that his prospective employee must make an advantage out of the obvious disadvantage of being an Asian outsider within the U.S. marketplace. He thus decides on an appropriate sales image for Han: "A fine clean Christian young Oriental earning his way through college" (143).

In the Protestant tradition of the self-made man, Lively teaches that making money is a means of fulfilling a Christian calling: "in salesmanship, just as in Life, you must have Faith. Faith in all the finer, nobler things—in yourself, in the goods you are selling" (145). Using his Sunday School voice and a chalkboard, he opens the training session for his new employees with a lesson in climbing the ladder of success. Lively instructs his students to follow the "four S's," which he places in ascending order on the blackboard. The first "S" stands for Service: "Doing good is the secret of how [our company] makes money." The middle two "S's" stand for Stuff and Sticking, the necessary ingredients to completing the fourth "S": "Sales, of course!" exclaims Lively. "And it's sales that makes the successful man or woman in business." But, Lively insists, "it takes all four S's to make the big S in Success!" at which time he draws a line through all the S's and asks: "what do we get, folks? Why, yes! The American dollar!" Han's ecstatic response to Lively's instruction comes in the form of a rhetorical question: "Was I not being admitted into the Holy of Holies of the American civilization? This was just the very baptism I needed" (153–54).

Han's immersion in the fires of free enterprise is also the moment when he offers some of his most caustic, if unwitting, comments on the contradictions of the concept of success. The clerical tone of Lively's lecture inspires in his pupil a colonial frame of reference for understanding a sales vocation: "Almost like a missionary" (145), Han thinks, as he associates American capitalism with Christian charity in Korea. The narrator's knowledge of Chinese brings him to the unanticipated revelation: "I thought Mr. Lively would surely approve of the Chinese character for Buddha, which is man with a dollar sign after it (so: 佛)" (154). Here Han's familiarity with a non-Western language generates a poignant commentary on the enterprising man in America, for whom the Almighty Dollar is a manifestation of God's presence in this world.

Lively's assistant, Miss Fulton, reinforces her boss's lesson: "We are spreading the light of knowledge and a true foundation of good Christian character" (158). If nineteenth-century prophets of success preached that Mammon could serve God, their twentieth-century counterparts were known to contend that the salesman's winning personality might nourish the inner character of the customer. "We all know," Miss Fulton instructs, "that we are not only helping ourselves and the company . . . but we are making the customer do what we know is good for her" (158). Only the salesman willing to "revolutionize [his] personality" has the capacity to create desire and break down resistance: "The good salesman makes the customer want the unwanted article. . . . No customer willingly buys. He struggles against buying though it may be for his own good." Sporting a gold-toothed "successful smile," Miss Fulton urges her pupils: "Be vital, dynamic" and, above all, "make yourself an attractive human being" (154–56).

Although his door-to-door sales experience proves disastrous, Han, armed with personal magnetism, takes a job as a retail clerk in the chinaware section of a large department store chain in Philadelphia. He soon finds himself appalled by the management techniques employed by the company, which prompts his critique of Taylorization, the process by which human activity in the workplace is organized according to models of rational efficiency.[62] Han describes the enforced "regimentation" of department store work, where every employee has a number rather than a name and is governed by a clock, and sullenly concludes that "life in a department store was a horrible life for all people" (312–13). Work-related experiences of this sort force him to recognize that, despite his initial optimism, the work ethic in modern America "costs too much in soul-destroying energy" (318). Once he dreamed of becoming a department store buyer and climbing the corporate ladder of success (307). His enterprising vision is thwarted, however, when he is refused promotion from the level of a lowly sales clerk.[63] With the adverse experience behind him, Kang wrote in a 1941 autobiographical sketch: "I severed my commercial ties" forever.[64]

Han is haunted by the reality of racial prejudice directed at a nonwhite enterprising immigrant such as himself. "Once in America," he states near the conclusion of *East Goes West*, "I had a dream." It opens with the narrator climbing a lofty tree. Upon reaching its peak he sees a hairlike suspension bridge attached to a limb and stretching across a wide body of water to Korea, a nostalgic "paradise of wild and flowery magic . . . a never-never land." At the far end of the bridge, two of Han's boyhood friends beckon him to cross over. "But all in a moment, things began tumbling out of my pockets, money and keys, contracts and business letters. Especially the key to my car, my American car. I clutched, but I saw it falling" (400). The dream stages the impossibility of simply bridging or harmonizing the beliefs and value systems of Eastern and Western cultures. It also reveals the persistent lure of materialism for the immigrant Han: "ever present in my mind [during the dream] was the urgency of finding the car key, of recovering all of the money" (401).

Han, wandering through his dream searching for his money and keys, finds himself running down steps into a cryptlike cellar beneath an unnamed American city. He is not alone. The other men in the cellar are frightened-looking Negroes. Peering through the iron grating above, Han sees red-faced men outside carrying clubs, knives, and torches, and realizes that the cellar is being attacked by an angry lynch mob. "And through the grating I saw the flaring torches being brought. And applied. Being shoved, crackling, through the gratings. I awoke like the phoenix out of a burst of flames" (401). In his dream, Han fares little better than black men such as Tom Moss, who were lynched by white racists for their enterprising ambitions. An earlier comment from Han's close friend, To Wan Kim, echoes throughout the former's horrible dream. "But money and power in New York are not for men of my race," Kim instructs Han, and continues: "Even if we succeeded, we would not be admired for that, but only hated and feared" (232).

It might be best to interpret Han's dream sequence within the context of a nonwhite immigrant's existence in racially segregated America. The dream is thus symbolic not merely of the clash between Western society and an Eastern value system. It also stages the life-threatening circumstances—specifically, lynchings—under which he and his compatriots labored. In this light, it is difficult to read the narrator's Eastern interpretation of his dream as anything but a distressing recuperation of what is otherwise an immigrant's dream turned nightmare. "I have remembered this dream, because according to Oriental interpretation, it is a dream of good omen. To be killed in a dream means success, and in particular death by fire augurs good fortune. This is supposed to be so, because death symbolizes in Buddhistic philosophy growth and rebirth and a happier reincarnation" (401). Perhaps an appropriate gloss on Han's dream interpretation can be found in an observation provided by author Sui Sin Far. In a short story published during the Progressive Era, her narrator comments on the limits of Asian success in the United States: "with true Chinese philosophy he had begun to reject realities and accept dreams as the stuff upon which to live. Life itself was hard, bitter, and disappointing. Only dreams are joyous and smiling."[65]

But what if we take Han at his word, and translate his unmaking at the hands of an angry mob as a paragon of his phoenixlike resurrection?[66] His Oriental dream interpretation is drawn from the Buddhist belief in rebirth, a process that can take place after death or during life.[67] In The Grass Roof, the reader learns that Kang's autobiographical narrator was instructed in this philosophy during his boyhood days in Korea.[68] In the passage cited earlier, Han glosses the dream images with the Buddha's "fire sermon," which teaches that all emotional and physical possessions burn with the fires of attachment, hatred, and delusion. A goal of Buddha's instruction is the destruction of these three fires or defilements through Nirvana (literally meaning extinction or quenching). If Han has reached Nirvana, it is not so much a state of nothingness as a state of enlightened comprehension beyond understanding.

This opens an alternative reading of Han's dream interpretation, one perhaps less convincing but that nonetheless addresses the productivity of a nonwhite immigrant's frustrated efforts at free enterprise. By shifting his narrator's frame of reference to Buddhism, Kang generates an ethnic critique of the presuppositions behind the self-made man in America. The Western concept of the modern individual—particularly in the guise of the self-made man—is antithetical to teachings, which promote the concept of the "not-self." In a practical sense, the notion of the not-self is used to discourage attachment. On a spiritual level, it invites the idea that all things are impermanent and that, by implication, the true or empirical self does not exist. The goal of the Buddhist path is the relinquishing of emotional and material self-interest, and the attainment of a state of Nirvana that, while it is beyond impermanence, remains not-self.

Han's final recourse to a Buddhist frame of reference allows him to manage, if only imaginatively, some of the most pernicious obstacles blocking the immigrant's path not just to self-made success but to survival in the New World. More broadly, his interpretation of his nightmare bears witness to what, earlier in the novel, he identified as the "signs" of "this strangely great age of disintegration and new combination" between East and West (341). Ethnic identities are best understood, I believe, by the dialectical process through which the transplanted self is transformed by contact with the New World while challenging conventional standards for what it means to be American. In *East Goes West*, it is precisely at the crossroads—where East *meets* West—that Han hazards to affirm the efficacy of a modern ethnic identity.

5

Individual Enterprise in the Postfrontier Nation

Not-Quite-White Enterprise in the Tribal Twenties: *The Great Gatsby*

Prior to the consolidation of post–World War II corporate culture, and even before the onset of the Great Depression, the traditional figure of the self-made man in America was nearing its end. *The Great Gatsby* represents the diminishing moral authority of uplift stories in an age of declining faith in the nation's ability to assimilate new immigrants. Through the eyes of Fitzgerald's narrator, Nick Carraway, Gatsby appears in the guise of the archetypal, if somewhat misguided, self-made man. Gatsby's upward struggle is inspired by traditional purveyors of middle-class success, such as Ben Franklin and Horatio Alger. However, another less virtuous narrative of Gatsby's self-making unfolds, which connects his business schemes to the tainted hand of immigrant gangsters. A story of entrepreneurial corruption, accented by the language of nativism, competes with and ultimately foils the traditional narrative of virtuous ambitions. *Gatsby* thus stages a national anxiety about immigration and racial integration in the 1920s, an unease manifested in the crisis of the self-made man.

The Tribal Twenties produced the conditions under which Fitzgerald's narrator imagines Gatsby as a figure for America. Nick informs the reader in the opening pages that, despite his hero's criminal connections, "Gatsby turned out all right at the end."[1] In order to fulfill this expectation, the novel's famous conclusion must elide the narrative struggle—perpetrated by Gatsby's nativist rival, Tom Buchanan—over the ethnic as well as the ethical nature of our hero's enterprise. On the book's final page, Tom's interrogation into Gatsby's clouded past is displaced by Nick's inspirational vision of Gatsby's inviolate dream of the New World. The narrator conceives a myth of American origins by imagining initial contact with a virgin continent through "Dutch sailors' eyes" (189). Through this incarnation Gatsby becomes great: a forward-looking visionary who not only transcends the crisis of his contemporary moment but who is also associated with the nation's legendary pastoral promise.

Lionel Trilling's statement that Gatsby "comes inevitably to stand for America itself" best exemplifies the consensus among Fitzgerald critics who have, over the past fifty years, turned *The Great Gatsby* into *the* novel of the American dream.[2] This sentiment, I believe, carries with it residual (albeit unwitting) traces of 1920s nativism that are embedded in the book's ending. One of the earliest critics to identify the theme of the American dream in *The Great Gatsby* was Edwin Fussell. In "Fitzgerald's Brave New World," he suggests that Gatsby is corrupted "by values and attitudes that he holds in common with the society that destroys him." Within a "mechanized" world, Fussell points out that "a dream like Gatsby's cannot remain pristine, given the materials upon which the original impulse toward wonder must expend itself."[3]

Nevertheless, we are left with a persistent question. Despite mounting evidence supporting Tom's accusations regarding his rival's entrepreneurial corruption through shady associations with immigrant gangsters, how does Gatsby maintain "his incorruptible dream" (162) in the eyes of the narrator and readers alike? The standard procedure among critics is to interpret Gatsby's dream according to Nick's narrative demands: like Nick, critics usually separate modern corruption from a pristine dream located in the nation's distant past. This type of commentary reads *Gatsby* according to an opposition between present and past, between Gatsby's unethical business connections and the wonder he inspires.[4] Marius Bewley, in his "Scott Fitzgerald's Criticism of America," was one of the first commentators to use this now widespread formulation. "The theme of *Gatsby*," Bewley states, "is the withering of the American dream" in industrial society. "We recognize that the great achievement of this novel," he concludes, "is that it manages, while poetically evoking a sense of the goodness of that early dream, to offer the most damaging criticism of . . . deficiencies inherent in contemporary manifestations of the American vision itself."[5] It is important to recognize that Fussell's and Bewley's interpretative models share the assumption that Gatsby's dream is principally a product of the past. These critics assume that the emergence of the American dream is coterminous with either the European discoveries of the New World, the seventeenth-century settlements along the eastern seaboard of North America, or the birth of the United States as a nation in the late eighteenth century.

Alternatively, I want to argue that the "American dream" is not a transhistorical concept but a term invented *after* the 1920s. As I discuss in the next section of this chapter, from the viewpoint of the Great Depression, the idea of the American dream addressed the moral vacuity of entrepreneurial self-making in the nation's past. In addition, the social climate of the early twenties, specifically as it is expressed in increasingly racialized forms of nativism, generated circumstances under which Nick remembers Gatsby as the representative American. Gatsby's dream does not have its origins in an earlier era of American history but is a product of the Tribal Twenties. This latter point builds on the provocative work of Walter Benn Michaels, who situates American national literature of the period, including *Gatsby*, within a discourse of nativism. However, Michaels's singular focus on nativism in the work of Fitzgerald and other canonical writers— exemplified in the statement, "What is to be feared most [in classic fiction of the 1920s] is the foreigner's desire to become American"— elides the persistence of racial segregation in this literature.[6] I argue that when the specter of black/white integration emerges in *Gatsby*, the rising tide of hostility toward new immigrants recedes.

Fitzgerald's novel reveals the degree to which, even for an uncompromising nativist such as Tom Buchanan, the transgression of black/white difference remains the most profound threat to the preservation of the country's Nordic identity. This threat is embedded, for instance, in the nativist myth of national origins. Nordicists, in assigning the role of New World discoverer to northern Europeans from Leif Eriksson to Henry Hudson, systematically excluded the introduction of black slaves from the beginning. The founding contributions of Africans in North America are not missing from a nativist history as a mere oversight. Their exclusion is symptomatic of how black/white difference was enforced through racial segregation during the twenties.

At first glance, nothing seems more remote from *The Great Gatsby* than the issue of racial segregation or black empowerment. Despite the novel's being set in metropolitan New York, African Americans almost never appear in Gatsby's world. Yet, from Garveyism to the fledgling Harlem Renaissance, New York was becoming the mecca of black American politics and culture. The near-complete absence of blacks from the novel can be comprehended only if we factor in the ubiquitous power of racial segregation. It is precisely the absence of African Americans alongside the novel's conspicuous appropriation of black culture that makes it a definitive text of the so-called Jazz Age.

In Nick's eyes Gatsby lives on the edge of two worlds, neither of which is black: the established white society of the Buchanans and the not-quite-white immigrant underworld of Meyer Wolfshiem. Yet Nick is at home in neither environment, a feeling reflected in his precarious sense of moral order in society. It is precisely the homeless perspective coupled with the ambivalent narrative expression of racial politics that places *Gatsby* squarely within the high modernist literary tradition. Like the work of Joseph Conrad, to which Fitzgerald acknowledged a primary debt, *Gatsby* undermines contemporary forms of racism only to the degree that it maintains them.[7] Although Nick consistently dismisses Tom Buchanan's racial nativism as "impassioned gibberish" (137), his own narration reinforces both the stereotypical degeneracy of the new immigrant (especially the Semite) and the minstrelsy of the Negro.

If blacks are conspicuous in their absence from Fitzgerald's Jazz Age fiction, there are notable exceptions that provide us ways of reading the persistent tension between black and white in the 1920s. African Americans appear at two crucial moments in the novel, both involving Gatsby's famed automobile: during Nick's memorable ride across the Queensboro Bridge and at the moment of the hit-and-run killing of Myrtle Wilson. Each scene, in its own way, anticipates Nick's concluding invocation of Gatsby's capacity for "wonder" in the Dutch sailors' eyes. In both instances new immigrants play a prominent role. In the latter (and, for our purposes, less significant) scene, a "pale, well-dressed Negro" is described as the one person able to identify accurately the "death car" as Gatsby's. Interestingly enough, the only other witness to the hit-and-run accident is the "young Greek, Michaelis" (144–47).

In the Queensboro Bridge scene, immigrants and blacks are not passive witnesses to Gatsby and his gilded machine. Instead they share the American road with him. As Nick rides beside Gatsby and experiences the "wonder" associated with "the city seen for the first time, in its first wild promise" (73), an immigrant funeral procession passes. Our narrator observes that the deceased's "friends looked out at us with the tragic eyes and short upper lips of south-eastern Europe." Here, Nick marks these immigrants as emotionally and physically distinct from old stock Americans. However, by cheerfully adding that his hero's "splendid car was included in their somber holiday" (73), Nick implies that the distance between Gatsby's world and that of the immigrant is not so great after all. The Queensboro Bridge excursion immediately precedes Nick's introduction to Gatsby's business associate, Meyer Wolfshiem, the Jewish gangster characterized by stereotypical Semitic features.

Before Nick and Gatsby reach their noon engagement with Wolfshiem, another car overtakes them on the Queensboro Bridge. It is a limousine, "driven by a white chauffeur, in which sat three modish Negroes, two bucks and a girl." In contrast to the funeral procession, the narrator finds this scene intensely amusing: "I laughed aloud as the yolks of their eyeballs rolled toward us in haughty rivalry" (73). Beyond the obvious racial stereotyping of the happy darkies aping white ways, note the pleasure Nick takes in observing the high-spirited Negroes, an amusement indebted to the legacy of blackface minstrelsy in the United States.[8] The reflection of the sportive

Negroes in Gatsby's "mirrored" (68) car—rather than their inclusion in his world—illustrates how the color line fixes the separation between blacks and whites even as it generates an ambivalent identity between the two.

Racial segregation, by excluding African Americans from full participation in U.S. society, managed the challenge that blacks posed to white supremacy in the economic marketplace and elsewhere. When, during the 1920s, black empowerment threatened white privilege, nationalists readily abandoned their nativist attack on non-Nordic Europeans and reasserted the need for black/white separation through appeals to (among other things) intrawhite brotherhood. A case in point was President Warren Harding's widely publicized speech before a racially mixed audience in Birmingham, Alabama, in November 1921. Harding was an influential post–Progressive Era nativist. Upon entering office, he immediately overturned former President Woodrow Wilson's veto of an immigration restriction bill. The temporary law, according to one historian, "proved in the long run the most important turning-point in American immigration policy."[9] In his fall speech before the Southern city of Birmingham, Harding conveniently repressed his nativist platform. Lecturing on behalf of "the self respect of the colored race," the president argued for maintaining the "natural segregations" between black and white. Without hesitation, he turned to the white audience and pleaded for national unity: "The one thing we must sedulously avoid is the development of group and class organizations in this country" based on "the labor vote, the business vote, the Irish vote, the Scandinavian vote, the Italian vote, and so on."[10] Clearly, here was a prominent American who, while supporting nativist demands for restricting immigration from southeastern Europe, appealed to intrawhite brotherhood when the specter of desegregation was raised.

Black intellectual W. E. B. Du Bois, who once described "the problem of the Twentieth century" as "the color-line," was outraged by what he called "the logical contradictions" of the president's address. In order to illustrate his point, he used his December editorial in the NAACP's *Crisis* magazine to place the contradictory statements side by side. Harding promoted black/white segregation while, in the same breath, criticizing "demagogues" who pitted old stock white Americans against recent European immigrants. Du Bois thus asked rhetorically: "Is the President calling himself a demagogue?" He countered the president's statements by offering a twofold warning to "Harding or any white man" about teaching "Negroes pride of race." First, "our pride is our business and not theirs." Second, black pride is something whites "would better fear rather than evoke." Du Bois concluded apocalyptically: "For the day that Black men love Black men simply because they are Black, is the day they will hate White men simply because they are White. And then, God help us all!"[11]

Du Bois was making a thinly veiled reference to his political rival, Marcus Garvey, the Jamaican-born nationalist leader who based his United Negro Improvement Association headquarters in Harlem. In late 1921, Garvey was reaching the peak of his popularity among the black masses. A few months earlier he had publicly chastised "the Dr. Du Bois group" for fighting racial segregation. In opposition, Garvey reiterated the UNIA's belief that "amalgamation . . . is a crime against nature." Writing in a November 1921 issue of the UNIA newspaper *Negro World*, he heaped praise upon President Harding for the "Great Vision" conveyed in his Birmingham address and urged blacks to stand together "against the idea of social equality."[12]

Garvey built the first and largest mass movement ever among blacks in the United States by, in part, conceding that "America [is] a White Man's Country" and exploiting the racist assertion as a means of promoting his enterprising Back-to-Africa campaign. After 1922, a period marked by Garvey's declining political fortunes, the UNIA leader openly flirted with white racist and nativist groups, ranging from the Ku Klux Klan to the Anglo-Saxon Clubs of America. However, public overtures to white supremacists did little to stop the federal government from arresting the UNIA leader on mail fraud charges and jailing him in 1923 and between 1925 and 1927. Even the vague threat posed by Garvey's unprecedented ability to mobilize large numbers of blacks forced the U.S. government to deport him immediately upon his release from prison. Garvey was both black and an immigrant in an era of intense hostility toward both groups. However, his nationalist dream of a distant but glorious African past was not far from being the black mirror image of Gatsby's timeless dream of northern European national origins in Dutch explorers' eyes. Both visions were a part of the politics of immigration restriction and racial segregation in New York City during the twenties.

Higham reports that around 1920 Nordicists began attacking new immigrants—particularly Catholics and Jews, but Japanese on the Pacific Coast as well—under a nativist banner that now tied racial to more traditional religious xenophobia. Before the end of the year, the gathering tide of anti-immigration sentiment became fueled by both an economic downturn and a sharp increase in the importation of cheap labor from abroad. These twin factors—the state of the economy and the scale of immigration—regularly play a role in establishing the level of nativism in the United States. However, Higham puts forward a third determinant in nativist politics that exploded on the scene in 1920 and assumed greater importance than ever before: namely, the connection between foreigners and crime.[13] The conflation of new arrivals with unethical business practices offers the license for reading *The Great Gatsby* according to the rise of nativism and the fall of the self-made man.

Fitzgerald's familiarity with the grammar of nativism was likely informed by his professional affiliation during the 1920s with the *Saturday Evening Post*. During this period, he placed many of his short stories with the *Post* and, as such, it became his most lucrative source of income while composing *Gatsby*. As the nation's most popular magazine, the *Post* began publishing nativist opinions in its pages as early as the spring of 1920. At this time *Post* editorials advocated the racialist doctrines of Madison Grant. During the same year, its editor, George Horace Lorimer, sent Kenneth Roberts abroad to report on European immigration to the United States. According to Higham, Roberts's articles (which appeared in the *Post* and which were published in a 1922 collection under the title *Why Europe Leaves Home*) became the most widely read effusions on Nordic theory of its day.[14] Roberts began from the twin premises of Nordicism: "The American nation was founded and developed by the Nordic race" and "Races can not be cross-bred without mongrelization." Writing overseas, he speculated that "if a few more million members of the

Alpine, Mediterranean and Semitic races are poured among us, the result must inevitably be a hybrid race of people as worthless and futile as the good-for-nothing mongrels of Central America and Southeastern Europe."[15]

Early in *Gatsby*, Tom Buchanan, working himself into a frenzy about the threat of mongrelization to the nation's white identity, whispers to the dinner guests at his Long Island estate: "The idea is that we're Nordics . . . and we've produced all the things that go to make civilization" (18). Tom's words remind us that Nordicism was a form of nativism activated in post–World War I America. In its everyday expressions, Nordicism conflated Saxons (English), Dutch (Germans), as well as Nordics (Scandinavians), despite the fact that these immigrant groups did not always have an amicable coexistence on the North American continent. The popular appeal of Nordicism during the twenties provides a context for understanding the production of classic American literature at mid-decade. For example, William Carlos Williams's relocation of the discovery of America in the voyages of "Red Eric" (father of Leif Eriksson) in the opening pages of *In the American Grain* (1925) might signal something more than the anti-Puritan impulse common to writers of this era. Fitzgerald's Dutchmen, like Williams's Norsemen, bear the inadvertent mark of nativism specific to the twenties. Nick's invocation of the Dutch sailors' vision of the New World adheres to the nativist logic of President Coolidge's April 1924 message to Congress on passage of the immigration bill: "America must be kept American."[16]

The discourse of Nordicism circulated in academic and popular forums alike. For instance, during the same month and year as the president's congressional address, an argument for Nordic superiority appeared in a letter to the editor of the *New York Times*, signed by Henry Fairfield Osborn. Its author, a prominent biologist and president of both the American Museum of Natural History and the Second (1921) International Congress of Eugenics, proposed that "the selection, preservation and multiplication of the best heredity is a patriotic duty of first importance." A dozen years earlier, at the height of the Progressive Era, Columbus Day was officially introduced as a holiday in New York. Attempting to make sense of the current "confusion between nationality and race," Osborn points out that "Columbus, from his portraits and from his busts, authentic or not, was clearly of Nordic ancestry." For Osborn, tracing bloodlines of racial descent was the key to ending the confusion over the identity of the "discoverer" of New World America.

The Nordic debate over Columbus's place in American history emerged in the *New York Times* as early as the summer of 1922, when Fitzgerald began composing short stories that would lead to *Gatsby* and at the moment when he stages the initial encounter between Nick and Gatsby on Long Island. Now a backlash in public opinion raged on the editorial pages of the *Times*. A letter dated 23 June 1922 opened by congratulating the newspaper for its "fine editorials . . . against perverted historical facts tending to encourage Anglo-phobia." The author proposed "the elimination of the Columbus legend" in light of recent discoveries that "reveal the real America, discovered by . . . Leif Erikson, from whose strong Nordic stock our early pioneers derived their rugged virtues."[17] The nativist proposal drew a response in a *Times* letter, dated June 30, from the editor of a journal published by the Knights of Columbus. Although the author acknowledged "Ericson's arrival" in the New World, he complains: "At present there is a persistent and extremely verbose propaganda seeking to diminish the achievement of Columbus."[18] Not surprisingly, counterresponses ensued, including one dated July 4 under the title "Leif Did Discover America!" and signed "Nordic." The letter, which followed the logic of Nordicism by conflating immigrants of English and Scandinavian descent, insisted that "Americans of Anglo-Saxon lineage are glad to know that . . . one of their own Nordic strain, was the real discoverer of this continent." Clinton Stoddard Burr summed up the nativist tone of the *Times* with his 1922 proclamation: "Americanism is actually the racial thought of the Nordic race."[19]

Gatsby's association with immigrant crime, particularly in the form of bootlegging, jeopardizes both the purity of his white identity and the ethics of his entrepreneurial success. The association of immigrants with lawlessness was crystallized during Prohibition, which was no less than a moral crusade to preserve the American Way through social control and conformity. The Eighteenth Amendment propelled organized gangsterism to new heights and, in doing so, opened opportunities for new arrivals by creating a lucrative trade in illicit alcohol. It also activated the stereotype of the nonnorthern European immigrant as gangster, realized in sensational trials such as that of "Bootleg King" millionaire Harry Brolaski who, in his own words, "always took a gambling chance." In four months from June to September 1920, Brolaski made a fortune that was lost before the end of the year when he was tried and convicted of masterminding a Pacific Coast bootlegging ring.[20]

Despite the fact that Gatsby's original surname ("Gatz") carries a possible Jewish inflection, there is little if any evidence to support the claim that the protagonist is the offspring of recent immigrants. Nevertheless, he is undoubtedly a bootlegger who associates with unsavory new arrivals and vile members of the underworld. The association forces him to make up improbable stories about his past because, as he explains to Nick, "I didn't want you to think I was just some nobody" (71). Although Nick desperately wants to believe in Gatsby's grand self-descriptions, contemporary reviewers were not always so sympathetic. One insists that the "Great Gatsby wasn't great at all—just a sordid, cheap, little crook."[21] Information marshaled by Tom Buchanan's investigation into Gatsby's past supports such a reading:

> "Who are you anyhow?" broke out Tom. "You're one of that bunch that hangs around with Meyer Wolfshiem—that much I happen to know. I've made a little investigation into your affairs . . . I found out what your 'drug stores' were." He turned to us and spoke rapidly. "He and this Wolfshiem bought up a lot of side-street drug stores here and in Chicago and sold grain alcohol over the counter. That's one of his little stunts. I picked him for a bootlegger the first time I saw him and I wasn't far wrong." (141)

Gatsby brazenly refuses to deny Tom's accusation of his bootlegging activities, responding politely: "What about it? . . . I guess your friend Walter Chase wasn't too proud to come in on it." Tom's findings not only implicate his rival in various unnamed criminal schemes by providing almost irrefutable evidence of his involvement in the illegal sale of alcohol. Hoping to play to the nativist fears of his audience, he also binds Gatsby's identity to the Jewish gangster Wolfshiem.

Nick's stereotypical description of Wolfshiem is colored by racial nativism to the extent that it carries with it traces of the degeneracy associated with Semites. Upon being introduced by Gatsby to his friend, the narrator provides the following description of Wolfshiem: "A small flat-nosed Jew raised his large head and regarded me with two fine growths of hair which luxuriated in either nostril. After a moment I discovered his tiny eyes in the half darkness." Nick repeatedly characterizes the man he finds "looking for a business gonnegtion" according to his gross physical appearance, typified by references to "his tragic nose" (73–77). The descriptions implicate Nick in a form of what Sander Gilman calls "pathological stereotyping."[22] Immutable stereotyping of this sort licenses the construction of a rigid difference between the vigorous Anglo-Saxon, Tom Buchanan, and degenerate Jew Meyer Wolfshiem. Gatsby is caught in a no-man's-land between the two ethnic extremes.

Wolfshiem's business activities are not merely illegal; they threaten the integrity of the national sporting event, baseball's World Series. Eventually we learn that he runs his illicit business out of "The Swastika Holding Company," a name that continues to befuddle readers. It is unlikely that Fitzgerald would have known that Hitler was using the swastika as the symbol of his fledgling Nazi party. Instead, the swastika was widely recognized at the time as an ancient Aryan symbol of good luck.[23] Wolfshiem's possession of the swastika as the name of his holding company manifests the widely perceived threat to an Aryan nation posed by enterprising immigrants, particularly Jews. Burr, in his book *America's Race Heritage* (1922), insists that the "most objectionable classes of the 'new' immigration are rapidly breaking down American institutions and honorable business methods." In the context of discussing recent Jewish arrivals, he describes "business trickery" as a "trait . . . so ingrained that one may doubt whether it could be eradicated for generations."[24]

Gatsby's illicit business association (indeed, his friendship) with immigrant gangster Meyer Wolfshiem compromises the ethics of self-made success while undermining the stability of white ethnic difference. His enterprising efforts among shady foreigners stages the nation's growing suspicion of immigrants after World War I. This sentiment is confirmed, for instance, in a contemporary commentator's use of an anti-Catholic slur to describe Gatsby upon his first encounter with Daisy. Thomas Chubb, in his review of the novel in the August 1925 issue of *Forum* magazine, commented that Gatsby "is still poor as an Irishman on Sunday morning."[25] Even Nick, after meeting his mysterious neighbor for the first time at one of his gala parties, immediately thinks of his host as a stranger in his own home: "I would have accepted without question the information that Gatsby sprang from the swamps of Louisiana or from the lower East Side of New York" (54).

Nick's suspicions about the source of Gatsby's wealth are heightened just after he is introduced to Wolfshiem. Gatsby is caught off guard and becomes noticeably upset when, having boasted that it took him only three years to earn his fortune, Nick points out that he was under the impression that he had "inherited" his money through a legacy of family wealth (95). In the chapter that follows this uneasy exchange, Nick casts young Jimmy Gatz in the role of an Alger boy-hero who had a fortunate encounter with wealthy yachtsman Dan Cody.[26] Yet Nick's telling of Gatsby's "luck and pluck" tale suggests the loss of faith in stories of the self-made man at this time. For example, Gatsby's benefactor, Cody, is not the genteel aristocrat of Alger's stories but "the pioneer debauchee." He is a product of "the savage violence of the frontier brothel and saloon," and thus a considerable distance from even the celebrated frontier individualist imagined by Progressive Era historian Frederick Jackson Turner. When he sets sail for the West Indies and the Barbary Coast (places associated with pirating, the African slave trade, and colonialism), Cody employs the impressionable teenager in some "vague personal capacity" and gives him a "singularly appropriate education" before dying suddenly (106–7). Fitzgerald's peculiar appropriation of the Alger formula suggests a crisis in the traditional narrative of character-based uplift. Recall that, only a decade prior to the publication of *Gatsby*, melting-pot advocate Mary Antin proclaimed that the modern self-made man started at the bottom of the overseas ship's steerage. During the 1920s, the idea of virtuous immigrant enterprise was undercut by a declining commitment to assimilating new arrivals.

After Gatsby's own sudden death, Nick approaches Wolfshiem—the deceased's "closest friend"—for an account of Gatsby's source of wealth. Wolfshiem's recollection functions to reconfirm the new threat the immigrants posed to ethical entrepreneurship. To Nick's inquiry, "Did you start him in business?" Wolfshiem replies, "Start him! I made him," and continues: "I raised him up out of nothing, right out of the gutter. I saw right away he was a fine appearing gentlemanly young man and when he told me he was an Oggsford I knew I could use him good. . . . We were so thick like that in everything—" He held up two bulbous fingers "—always together" (179). Wolfshiem's depiction of Gatsby's uplift helps confirm the findings of Tom's investigation. Not only is Gatsby "raised . . . up out of nothing," he is "made" not by the sweat of his honest brow but by the black hand of the immigrant gangster. Wolfshiem's grotesque "bulbous fingers" offer a degenerate image of togetherness. If he and Gatsby are as separate as fingers, they are also as one as the hand. Wolfshiem's story of Gatsby's inauspicious beginnings leaves Nick wondering whether their "partnership" also included the World's Series scandal.

The encounter with Wolfshiem immediately leads to another illustration of Gatsby's original ambition, one apparently modeled on the prescriptions of middle-class morality. This example takes a page out of Benjamin Franklin's autobiography. However, because it mocks the conventions of character building associated with the tradition of self-made success, this illustration ultimately functions to undermine evidence for Gatsby's wholesome uplift. More specifically, the reader is presented with Jimmy Gatz's transcription, on the flyleaf of a dime novel, of a Franklin-style timetable and resolves.[27] Unlike Franklin, who builds the "perfect Character" by pondering questions of inner goodness before setting out for a day of hard work, sixteen-year-old Gatsby's morning itinerary and daily resolves are essentially devoid of the art of virtue. Instead of nourishing his soul, young Gatsby reshapes his body through "Dumbbell exercise and wall-scaling" and betters his mind by "read[ing] one improving book or magazine per week" (181–82). If the former suggests a heightened regard for superficial self-improvement in this century, the latter invokes the currents of New Thought. "The development of 'mind-power,'" Richard Weiss properly explains, "occupied the same position in the new literature of self-help that the development of character had in the old."[28] In the end, Fitzgerald offers a twentieth-century parody of Franklin's archetypal self-made man. More specifically, Gatsby's self-advancement demonstrates the extent to which, with the consolidation of consumer society, the cult of personality eclipsed an earlier producer-oriented notion of character. The defection from character did not single-handedly undermine the traditional narrative of success. However, when coupled with rising suspicions regarding both the rectitude of new immigrants and popular get-rich-quick schemes, the apparent excesses of the personality craze contributed to the diminishing authority of the figure of the self-made man during the 1920s. Fitzgerald represented this national identity crisis through Gatsby.

The social climate that guaranteed Gatsby's failure as the traditional self-made man also provided the social conditions under which his pristine dream could be imagined. During the twenties, racial nativism was sanctioned by the pseudoscientific discourse of Nordicism, which narrowed definitions of whiteness. After decades of seemingly unrestricted immigration from eastern and southern Europe, nativists responded to the fear of the loss of white supremacy by attempting to fix and maintain the boundaries between Americans of northwestern European descent and all others. Higham explains that the deployment of genetic typologies became widespread in Nordicist descriptions of the racial degeneracy in new immigrants. Respectable social scientist Madison Grant, probably the most important nativist in modern American history,[29] worked from the "science" of eugenics and taught two basic lessons. First, old stock Americans should properly identify themselves as Nordic. Second, Nordics must avoid cross-breeding with white Europeans of a lower racial descent, namely, Alpines and Mediterraneans, or face the degenerative process of "mongrelization."[30]

Gatsby's romantic ambition is, of course, to amass a fortune fantastic enough to win the heart of Daisy Fay, who reveals that she is as much Southern belle as flapper when she refers to her own youth as her "white girlhood" (24). A consumerist version of the all-American girl, Daisy is a symbol for a Nordic national identity in the twenties.[31] She functions within the novel as a gendered sign for the mythological American continent: a nurturing mother and a beckoning lover who offers "the incomparable milk of wonder" (112). The fact that Daisy's voice is also described as "full of money—that was the inexhaustible charm that rose and fell in it" (120) is less a contradiction than the other side of the same coin. In an era of neocolonial corporate expansion, the frontier is seductive not in spite of but because of its exploitability. At the novel's conclusion, Daisy's green light in Gatsby's eyes invokes, for Nick, the Dutch explorers' initial sighting of a pristine America.

Paradoxically, Gatsby must transgress the Nordic/non-Nordic divide and associate with immigrant gangster Meyer Wolfshiem in order to generate a fortune grand enough to impress the belle of Louisville. In a desperate attempt to foil Gatsby's dazzling design, Tom spews the slogans and parrots the precepts of Nordic supremacy. It is no secret that Nordicism receives its most unrestrained expression on the pages of *Gatsby* in the voice of Tom Buchanan. As one contemporary reviewer of the novel reluctantly observed, Tom "is an American university product of almost unbearable reality."[32] Tom assaults Nick with his nativist racism early in the novel, before either one of them is introduced to Gatsby. Over dinner at the Buchanan Long Island estate, Nick confesses that his cosmopolitan cousin, Daisy, makes him feel "uncivilized." Before Daisy responds, Tom interrupts the conversation with a gloomy prediction: "Civilization's going to pieces. . . . I've gotten to be a terrible pessimist about things. Have you read 'The Rise of the Coloured Empires' by this man Goddard?" Nick answers in the negative, and Tom, in a petulant mood, approvingly explains the book's thesis: "The idea is if we don't look out the white race will be—will be utterly submerged. It's all scientific stuff; it's been proved" (17). The exchange has led literary critics to speculate that Tom's authority is Lothrop Stoddard, whose conservative ideas were widely disseminated among nativists after the publication of his *Rising Tide of Color*.[33]

Nativists voiced the fear that America's once pure racial stock was now under siege by a generation of unsavory immigrants who were, in too many instances, amassing wealth without adhering to the Protestant work ethic and the gospel of virtuous success.[34] "It's up to us who are the dominant race to watch out," asserts Tom, "or these other races will have control of things" (17). His sense of control is defined by his faith in the moral superiority of northern European civilization. Nick thinks to himself that Tom's white supremacist monologue is "pathetic." Daisy responds to her husband with little more than sarcasm ("We've got to beat them down"). Her friend, Jordon Baker, offers the most provocative, albeit cryptic, aside: "You ought to live in California—." Jordon's passing reference to the West Coast is made intelligible when we consider the politics of nativism in California at the time. After Japan demonstrated its military prowess in the Russo-Japanese War of 1904, Anglo-Americans on the Pacific Coast experienced a twofold threat: fears about Japan's expansionist foreign policy were placed alongside the danger Japanese immigration posed to Anglo hegemony on the West Coast.[35] Even Stoddard, who discusses the international "Yellow Peril" at length in *The Rising Tide of Color*, makes reference to the California crisis by quoting from the *Los Angeles Times*: "If California is to be preserved for the next generation as a 'white man's country' there must be some movement started that will restrict the Japanese birth-rate in California."[36] By the time of Harding's presidential election in 1920, anti-Japanese hysteria on the West Coast had reached unprecedented levels.[37] As a result, the Johnson-Reed Act was drafted in a way that prohibited Japanese immigration altogether, completing a long-standing policy of Oriental exclusion.

Tom, oblivious to criticism of almost any kind, interrupts Jordon's mention of California with the proposition that "we're Nordics" (18). Later, during the novel's climactic Plaza Hotel scene, Tom and Gatsby square off against one another. Tom, by linking Gatsby's enterprising ambitions to Wolfshiem's underworld operations, turns his personal claim on a Nordic identity into a weapon against his rival. In doing so, he diminishes Gatsby's standing in society to that of the "nobody" our hero so desperately wants to escape. "I suppose the latest thing is to sit back and let Mr. Nobody from Nowhere make love to your wife. . . . Nowadays people begin by sneering at family life and family institutions and next they'll throw everything overboard and have intermarriage between black and white" (137). This passage expresses the complex relation between nativism and the color line at the time. It is tempting to conclude, along with Walter Benn Michaels, that Tom is identifying Gatsby "as in some sense black."[38] But this would be to misjudge the degree to which, even during the twenties, nativists were willing or able to collapse the distinction between blacks and immigrants from southeastern Europe. According to the nativist logic of Tom's argument, Gatsby seems less than white because of his intimate connection with immigrant crime. The association licenses Tom's accusation that Gatsby jeopardizes the health of the family, the institution indispensable to maintaining white racial purity. Next, he suggests that black/white miscegenation poses the most profound threat to the Nordic race. Although Tom does not suggest that Gatsby is in any way black, his statement reveals the degree to which nativists narrowed the notion of whiteness while simultaneously maintaining what President Harding called the "natural segregations" between black and white.

Jordon Baker, in response to Tom's diatribe against Gatsby, makes another spontaneous intervention: "We're all white here." Jordon's comment points to a crisis in the nation's Nordic identity, where, for nativists at least, whiteness is no guarantee of racial purity. The fragility of the modern family—racial and national, extended and nuclear—was at the heart of nativist arguments against unrestricted immigration. Nordic nationalist Charles W. Gold, in a book titled *America: A Family Matter* (1922), attributed the downfall of Rome, and by extension "the continuing downfall of humanity" up through the present, to mongrelization. Although he appears to be unaware of the fact that the "melting pot" was a concept only recently popularized during the Progressive Era, Gold nonetheless argues that throughout the ages efforts at this type of ethnic assimilation have been misguided. "Tear from the phrase the softening metaphor and we recognize 'melting pot' in its true, its unpleasant form—'miscegenation.'" He concludes that national histories teach America a simple but indispensable lesson: "Repeal our naturalization laws." Legislative reform would bar entrance to aliens, helping to "secure our children and our children's children in their legitimate birthright."[39] Or, as Lothrop Stoddard pleaded, "the immigrant tide must at all costs be stopped and America given a chance to stabilize her ethnic being."[40] The passage of the Johnson-Reed Act in 1924 fulfilled the demands of racial nativists, who insisted on the preservation of what they regarded as a "distinct American type": the white northern European Protestant. The law implemented a "national origins" principle. By setting quotas according to the contribution of each national stock to the American population, the law ensured that six or seven times more immigrants would originate annually from northwestern Europe than from southeastern Europe. Higham concludes that, by counting everyone's ancestors, the Johnson-Reed Act "gave expression to the tribal mood, and comfort to the democratic conscience."[41]

The frequently cited conclusion of *The Great Gatsby* illustrates nationalism in its general form as well as its manifestation peculiar to the 1920s. Broadly speaking, Fitzgerald represents the double-sided logic of nationalism by offering, on the one hand, a promising future in the prophecy "tomorrow we will run faster, stretch out our arms farther" and, on the other, an immemorial myth of American national origins envisioned in "boats . . . borne back ceaselessly into the past" (189). I offer the final passage from Freud's *Interpretation of Dreams* as a gloss on Gatsby's pristine dream in the famous last lines of Fitzgerald's novel: "By picturing our wishes as fulfilled, dreams are after all leading us into the future. But this future, which the dreamer pictures as the present, has been moulded by his indestructible wish into a perfect likeness of the past."[42] Following Freud, we might say that Nick's belief in Gatsby's gift of hope for a more perfect future is inverted in the expression of his hero's vision of an inviolate past. Gatsby's Janus-faced wonder at "the orgiastic future that year by year recedes before us" is mirrored in the eyes of Nick's sixteenth-century Dutch explorers.[43]

In death Gatsby is freed from his venal partnership with immigrant gangsters and remembered within a lineage of northern European explorers. Fitzgerald might have returned his reader to the "Columbus story" (9), used near the beginning of the novel to map the geographical configuration of Gatsby's "ancestral home" (162). Instead, Nick resurrects his hero's fallen reputation by transforming Gatsby's glimpse at Daisy's green light into the desire in the "Dutch sailors' eyes" for the continent that "flowered" before them as "a fresh, green breast of the new world." Against the current wave of immigration, Gatsby is "borne back ceaselessly" into a northern European past as recollected within the nativist climate of the 1920s, when conceptions of whiteness both narrow and become a sign not of skin color but of national identity.

Inventing the American Dream in the Great Depression: *The Epic of America*

Despite half a century of literary criticism on the expression of the American dream in Fitzgerald's *Great Gatsby*, the phrase is a misnomer when used to characterize the book's nationalist vision. The term was not put into print until 1931, when middle-brow historian James Truslow Adams coined and used it throughout the pages of a book titled *The Epic of America*.[44] Adams's history of the United States was widely read; it was a Book-of-the-Month Club selection that ultimately topped the best-seller list in 1932.[45] The American dream is to be understood as an ethical doctrine that is symptomatic of a crisis in national identity during the thirties.[46] The newly invented dream calls out for a supplement to the outmoded narrative of individuated uplift, which had lost its moral capacity to guide the nation during the Depression. Adams makes no mention of Fitzgerald or *The Great Gatsby* in his book, nor should he. By explicitly appealing to a shared, rather than tribal, sense of national identity, he steers clear of group conflict and directs his reader toward a secular belief in the American dream. For Adams, the spirit of the dream invokes an ecstatic faith in the nation's heroic past and a willingness to sacrifice for its future.[47]

Adams's history marks the revival of communitarian concern in the thirties. He articulates his nationalist vision ("the American dream") through an ambiguous form of moral economics meant to address and subdue the imminent threat of class antagonism that was amplified by the Great Depression.[48] "The point is that if we are to have a rich and full life in which all are to share and play their parts, if the American dream is to be a reality, our communal spiritual and intellectual life must be distinctly higher than elsewhere, where classes and groups have their separate interests, habits, markets, arts, and lives."[49] The author's anticommunism is matched only by his anticonsumerism. Adams thus continues by placing the threat posed by socialism alongside that posed by the culture of consumption. "If the dream is not to prove possible of fulfillment, we might as well become stark realists, become once more class-conscious, and struggle as individuals or classes against one another. We cannot become a great democracy by giving ourselves up as individuals to selfishness, physical comfort, and cheap amusements" (411). Although Adams never explicitly critiques the popular concept of personality, such a criticism is implied in his objection to the increasing propensity for conspicuous consumption. The American dream, he concludes, "can never be wrought into a reality by cheap people or by 'keeping up with the Joneses'" (411).

Writing at the onset of the Depression, Adams's historical and moral vision was inspired by the Progressive Era.[50] For him, the period marked the most recent historical moment in which the promise of the American dream could be fulfilled. The thought of Frederick Jackson Turner, leading proponent of frontier mythology since the 1890s, is written across the pages of Adams's narrative.[51] The invention of the American dream was also indebted to the reformist impulses of muckraking. Adams was favorably impressed by the ethical component behind the journalistic exposés on the misdoing of corporate trusts: "America for the first time was beginning to take stock of the morality of its everyday business life" (353). Not surprisingly, he had nothing to say about the rise of enterprising women and minorities during the Age of Reform. Adams probably had never heard of Harriet Ayer or Madam Walker. Given that their success was lo-

cated within the new consumer markets—the very thing that supposedly contributed to the collapse of the American dream—it is
likely that he would have cast a skeptical eye across their contributions. Yet, Adams's blindness toward nontraditional entrepreneurs
helps explain his positive appropriation of Mary Antin's words from
The Promised Land at his book's end. Rather than cite from her discussion of her failed entrepreneurial ambitions, he quotes extensively
from her Emersonian vision of America past and future. Americans
in the Roaring Twenties, according to Adams, simply abandoned the
ideals of the Progressive Era: "The battle cries of Roosevelt and Wilson in the struggle to realize the American dream had been changed
into the . . . shouts for 'Coolidge prosperity'" (398). He asserts that
the get-rich-quick schemes of the 1920s coupled with consumerism
precipitated the near-complete bankruptcy of the American dream.

For Adams, the 1920s were not the origin of the dream's corruption, but rather its most recent manifestation. Adams locates the
source of the dream's demise in the rise of monopoly capitalism during the Gilded Age. In a chapter titled "The Age of the Dinosaurs,"
he deploys a discourse of natural history to describe the nation's de-
evolution from the Frontier Age to the "Jurassic period." Just as evo-
lutionary forces allowed huge and frightening reptiles to dominate
the earth in prehistoric times, "in our own age, a combination of elements suddenly brought into existence . . . huge business combina-
tions in the form of corporations of a hitherto undreamed-of size . . .
to rule the land." And, like the dinosaurs, whose extinction is attributed to a "lack of brain power," the author points to evidence for the
"difficulty of supplying our modern economic monsters with sufficient power of intellectual direction" (342–43). The incorporation of
America transformed the frontier town into a Jurassic industrial park
and reincarnated the exalted yeoman farmer as a self-interested robber baron. Adams lays the lion's share of the blame for the demise of
the dream at the feet of the nation's captains of industry, who not
only work in cahoots with corrupt government officials but lack the
requisite morality to ensure the country's spiritual as well as economic health. Instead of enshrining self-made men such as Carnegie,
Rockefeller, and Ford as the most recent purveyors of the American

dream, he sharply accuses them of betraying its very ideal. "To such men," asserts Adams, "the American dream was drivel" (347).

The Epic of America berates famous industrialists for allowing themselves to be "perniciously held up by newspapers and clergymen as models for ambitious American youth." Adams dismisses Alger-esque formulas exploited by businessmen in their autobiographies as little more than banal self-promotion, and concludes: "They did indeed have to have daring and courage, as does a pirate or a bootleg king, as well as ruthlessness" (315). Worse, U.S. citizens were currently placing the nation's destiny in the hands of men such as Henry Ford, who privileged practicality over morality: "Our most conspicuously successful manufacturer, Mr. Ford, announced in his new book in 1930 that 'we now know that anything which is economically right is also morally right.'" Adams criticizes Ford's statement by mocking his claim to an entrepreneurial form of statesmanship: "As the successful businessman would consider himself the best interpreter of good economics, he thus set himself up as the best judge of national morals" (400). The national ideal of manhood—the virtuous self-made man—proved to be a twentieth-century sham.

Adams insisted that the damage inflicted by the business elite on the nation was so great that it turned the American dream into a nightmare, a calamity currently being played out in the form of the Great Depression. His worst fears were probably confirmed when, only months after *The Epic of America* first appeared, a bloody battle between labor and capital erupted at the famous Ford River Rouge factory in Dearborn, Michigan. On 7 March 1932, a few thousand people, under the direction of the Communist Party USA, assembled at the Ford plant to make their demands known to management. Police were brought in to disperse the gathering and, by the end of the day, four demonstrators were killed and another fifty injured. For the general public prior to the Great Depression, River Rouge symbolized Ford—the beloved self-made hero and the successful company. By the early 1930s, however, the Ford name came to represent the utter incorrigibility of an entrepreneurial spirit past, while River Rouge conjured the ghosts of Homestead.

Adams's uncompromising criticism of once-glorified captains of industry found its full-blown expression in fellow historian Matthew Josephson's *Robber Barons*, a study that revealed the gross inequities of class in U.S. society. Unlike Josephson's study, however, which frequently reproduces the rags-to-riches formula in its biographies of industrialists and financiers, Adams's history had the distinction of not being held captive by the outmoded language of Horatio Alger uplift.[52] Regardless, the most thorough intervention into the idea of the virtuous self-made man probably was presented in the form of an American novel. In 1934, the same year *The Robber Barons* was published, Nathanael West's *A Cool Million* appeared. Its precursors can be found in the literary realism of Theodore Dreiser's *Sister Carrie* and Abraham Cahan's *The Rise of David Levinsky*. Although these Progressive Era novels are critical of the success ideal, the plight of their title characters nonetheless maintains many of the narrative conventions associated with rags-to-riches fiction. *A Cool Million* is different. For the first time, readers were offered an unyielding satire on moral luck and market pluck in the form of the literal dismemberment and reassemblage of the novel's protagonist, Lem Pitkin, in the name of shameless individual enterprise and corporate profit.[53]

Back in 1931, Adams was still left pondering the question, what is to be done? "It has been a great epic and a great dream," waxes the author at the end of his book. "What, now, of the future?" (405). Paradoxically, it was this present-tense query, directed at the nation's future, that underlies his narrative of U.S. history. Adams answers his own question with neither an ambitious economic road map nor a detailed legislative blueprint for recovery. Instead, *The Epic of America* maintains a secular faith in the communal concept of the American dream. Adams, I think, should be given credit for inventing an enduring national tradition, one that attempted to manage the social pressures of his contemporary moment (what he observed as the twin threats of communism and consumerism). In his popular history of the United States, he pointed to the source of these threats by addressing the moral hollowness of past self-made men.

6

The Ends of Self-Making

Image, Inc.: Howard Hughes, Lee Iacocca, and Ross Perot

If the appropriation of the language of individual enterprise by women, blacks, and immigrants delegitimated the traditional self-made man prior to 1930, the cold reality of the marketplace during the Great Depression made narratives of upward class mobility almost unimaginable. Yet Americans did not abandon self-culture. Instead, they looked away from narratives of enterprise and toward less monetary models for personal betterment. John Cawelti discovered that the thirties saw the proliferation of self-improvement manuals, such as Dale Carnegie's *How to Win Friends and Influence People* (1936) and Napoleon Hill's *Think and Grow Rich* (1937). These tracts rejected what had come to be known as the crass materialism behind the Alger formula in favor of prescriptions for positive thinking.[1]

However, when the economy pulled out of the Depression after World War II, the figure of the self-made man did not make a triumphant return. The recently consolidated corporate way of life appeared hostile to self-starters, and the loss of opportunities for individual enterprise was the price the nation had to pay for greater economic growth and stability. For David Riesman, author of *The Lonely Crowd* (1950), the work of Dale Carnegie marked the unfortunate displacement of the producer-oriented character by a consumer-oriented personality.[2] Three books appeared in 1956—William Whyte's

The Organization Man, C. Wright Mills's *The Power Elite*, and Robert L. Heilbroner's *The Quest for Wealth*—which essentially supported Riesman's evaluation. Each pondered what Heilbroner called "the dehumanization of the personality"[3] in corporate society, and each deployed (implicitly if not explicitly) ego-psychology to critique the acquisitive personality in postwar America.

Whyte, noting that "personality tests are the voice of The Organization,"[4] lamented the passing of individualistic ethos with the spread of conformity-minded big business. The changing face of enterprise gave Mills the confidence to conclude that "there is, in psychological fact, no such thing as a self-made man."[5] The author of *The Power Elite* exposed what he identified as the structural immorality behind corporate capitalism's anonymous facade: "In the corporate era, economic relations become impersonal—and the executive feels less personal responsibility." Not long ago, Mills observed, the entrepreneur—whether adored as a captain of industry or scorned as a robber baron—was at least in the public eye. After the Great Depression and World War II, business magnates were no longer "so visible as they once seemed." They had not been displaced, but instead were supplemented by a complex arrangement of corporate- and state-sponsored hierarchies that, worst of all, lacked genuine public accountability. Affluent industrialists "are still very much among us," Mills assured his reader, "even though many are hidden, as it were, in the impersonal organizations in which their power, their wealth, and their privileges are anchored."[6]

Howard Hughes, with his conspicuous disappearance from public view in 1957, became the most famous representative of the faceless corporate head and the new class of entrepreneurs. His story marks the end of traditional narratives of the self-made man. Because his business successes were founded on his sizable family inheritance, his life did not remotely fit the old-fashioned rags-to-riches scenario. As *Fortune* magazine was never tired of pointing out, Hughes was no Henry Ford.[7] Moreover, he was everything his father was not. Howard Senior was a moderately successful Texas oil man who invented a uniquely effective bit for drilling through rock for oil. Once the oil-drilling bit was patented in 1909, the Hughes family fortune

was guaranteed. As his son admitted in a rare autobiographical recollection, he failed to master the magnetic personality of his hardworking father:

> My father was plenty tough. He never suggested that I do some-
> thing; he just told me. He shoved things down my throat, and I
> had to like it. But he had a hail-fellow-well-met quality that I
> never had. . . . He was a terrifically loved man. I am not. I don't
> have the ability to win people the way he did. . . . I suppose I'm
> not like other men. Most of them like to study people. I'm not
> nearly as interested in people as I should be, I guess. What I am
> tremendously interested in is science, nature in its various manifes-
> tations, the earth and the minerals that come out of it.[8]

Here, in a 1948 interview, Hughes models his father's achievements
on a familiar formula for entrepreneurial success. The son even be-
trays a sense of guilt at not at least appearing to be interested in public relations and thus failing to measure up to the only available (albeit outmoded) models of self-made success.

Orphaned after his father's unexpected death in 1924, eighteen-
year-old Howard had the foresight to gain singular control of Hughes
Tool Company, and the good sense not to interfere with its day-to-
day operations.[9] Hughes's obsession with control—over his public
image as well as his corporate empire—became legendary. Although,
at one time, Hughes had made entrepreneurial forays into the emi-
nent world of Hollywood filmmaking, the shy executive exploited
the anonymity of the corporate structure and became known as "the
spook of American capitalism."[10] Slowly withdrawing from public
view throughout the fifties, Hughes, after 1957, vanished altogether.
He granted his last on-the-record interview in 1954 and, within two
years, instructed everyone, from the press to his top executives, not
to call him directly but to contact him through his Hollywood command post at 7000 Romaine Street. "What he really wants," his pub-
licist pleaded to an indifferent press corps in the early 1960s, "is to
have *nothing* written about himself."[11]

However, the proliferation of print and electronic media coupled
with the rise of the celebrity after World War II ensured that Hughes's
bid for complete anonymity would fail. A paradox, peculiar to the

logic of electronic image culture, thus emerged: the more Hughes demanded privacy, the more conspicuous became his presence in the media and the public imagination. From the late 1950s until his death in 1976, "Hughesiana" was a regular feature in magazines as diverse as *Fortune* and *Look*. It was not uncommon for editors to assign a star reporter to secure the exclusive Hughes interview; all, of course, were denied access.[12] Yet Hughes's secrecy simply fed the media's appetite for more information and the public's fascination with his reclusion. As a celebrity entrepreneur in absentia, he had a "visibility" that contemporary commentators on corporate life, such as C. Wright Mills, never anticipated.

At no time did Hughes compose an extended autobiographical statement regarding his personal life or professional achievements. To ensure his anonymity, he did his utmost to halt all biographies. By 1965, Hughes devised a legal means to protect his privacy: Rosemont Enterprises, Inc. Rosemont was set up by Hughes Tool Company executives and an independent contractor who worked outside his empire.[13] It was founded with one simple but unprecedented aim in mind: to patent a man's life in an effort to censor press speculation on Hughes himself. By claiming the exclusive rights to Hughes's personal history, Rosemont Enterprises attempted to foreclose the possibility that his story be made public through the mass media. It did so, for example, by buying the copyright on previously published magazine articles on him. Or, when a prospective biographer was preparing to go public with a book, Rosemont might make him an offer he could not refuse. In 1966, *Newsweek* reported that "at least two prospective biographers have disappeared into the ranks of [Hughes's] amorphous organization, never to be heard from again."[14]

Although only three biographies managed to slip by the Rosemont censors between 1966 and 1971, attempts at obstruction intensified tabloid speculation on the life and legend of Howard Hughes. However, in December 1971, the largest threat yet to his anonymity was posed. McGraw-Hill announced, with great fanfare, that it had secured the exclusive rights to his autobiography, which was scheduled for three-part serialization in *Life* magazine prior to the book's spring publication. According to the publisher's press release, Hughes had recently told his life story to a little-known American novelist named Clifford Irving. Hughes's executives immediately denounced the manuscript as an outright fraud. The denial proved ineffective, only fueling the book's prerelease publicity. Hughes, unable to halt the media tidal wave around the alleged "authentic autobiography," made a desperate gesture: he went public for the first time in fourteen years to make a personal disclaimer.[15] Rather than appear in the flesh before a ravenous press, he arranged a telephone conference call from his retreat in the Bahamas on 9 January 1972. The bizarre media event included seven journalists sitting in front of network television cameras inside a Los Angeles hotel room with the task of interviewing a disembodied voice transmitted from three thousand miles away.

To the astonishment of many listeners, Hughes not only rambled about obscure aeronautic technicalities but also failed to answer four of six initial "test" questions. The four unanswered questions had a common element: they asked him to identify particular individuals with whom he had had memorable contact in his early adulthood (for example, a superstitious woman who gave him a good-luck charm prior to his record-setting around-the-world flight, and a friend who had helped him construct an airplane engine). Hughes made almost no attempt to guess the correct answers to these nontechnical questions but, rather, simply stated: "I don't recall" and "I don't remember that."[16] As the authors of *Hoax*, the "inside" account of the Howard Hughes-Clifford Irving affair, observe: the interviewee's "weak point, it emerged, was people; his strong point hardware."[17] This alone leaves little doubt that the voice was indeed Hughes's.[18] After all, as his 1948 interview suggests, poor people skills and an obsession with technological detail had long been his trademark.

To Hughes's dismay, the telecommunicated press conference did little to put an end to the swirl of controversy surrounding the autobiography. Instead, it created a media circus that intensified public interest. The following Sunday, Mike Wallace interviewed Clifford Irving on *60 Minutes*. Before long, the *Los Angeles Times* had more reporters (nine) investigating the hoax than it had covering the Vietnam War. In order to capitalize on publicity and prevent "leaks," *Life* moved up the publication date of its exclusive excerpts from the autobiography.[19] Hughes's final bid for control over his anonymity failed because he and his advisers miscalculated the workings of an information society, which stages such spectacles not to squelch public interest but to generate it. As media theorists since Marshall McLuhan have known, the press does not merely report the news to us; it constructs our world as a media event. The momentary resurrection of Howard Hughes in front of a national audience made clear that, in a world increasingly transfixed by information and images, the press has the power to break as well as to make the subject of success.

The proliferation of the electronic media after World War II found a way to resurrect and repackage the idea of self-making by manufacturing and marketing the enterprising image through the charismatic figure of the celebrity. The media makes famous those enterprising individuals upon whom it confers an image of success. At the turn of the twenty-first century, the media-made personality is an image in search of an audience and a market share. *Iacocca* (1984), the blockbuster autobiography of the famous auto executive, illustrates the extent to which the preservation of the self-made man is an effect of corporate-media power. Consider the book's Prologue, where Lee Iacocca locates the origin of his celebrated success: "Fortunately, Chrysler recovered from its brush with death. Today I'm a hero. But strangely enough, it's all because of that moment of truth at the warehouse. With determination, with luck, and with help from lots of good people, I was able to rise up from the ashes."[20] At first glance, it appears that Iacocca simply offers his reader an old-fashioned "luck" and pluck ("determination") formula, adding a shade of modesty to balance his considerable ego. This indicates that, in the post–Civil Rights Era, where race relations shift and white ethnicity emerges as a trope of empowerment, an Italian American can inhabit an Anglo-Saxon narrative of moral luck.

The passage not only highlights the entrepreneur's good fortune and hard work. Iacocca also attributes his status as a hero to "that moment of truth at the warehouse." The life-defining event that transpired at the warehouse was his public burning before the news media on 16 October 1978, the day after his fifty-fourth birthday. According to Iacocca, this is the single most memorable experience of his life. Three months prior to the moment of truth, he had been fired as president of Ford Motor Company by its "despot" ruler, Henry Ford II. Now he was forced to flee Ford's palatial corporate headquarters in Dearborn for the confines of "an obscure warehouse" a few miles away. The press, however, preceded Iacocca to his place of exile, where it gathered to greet "the newly deposed president of Ford." Before he could find a place to park his car, an eager TV journalist shoved a microphone in his face and asked: "How do you feel, coming to this warehouse after eight years at the top?" Iacocca offered no comment, but the typical media inquiry demanded no response. In fact, it begged for reticence.[21] The television audience not only expected the moment of restless silence but sensed its significance. The refusal to comment confirms the media's presentation of the auto executive's descent down the corporate ladder.

What Iacocca identifies as his defining "moment of truth at the warehouse" was a media event staged not to endorse his heroic entrepreneurial stature but to ensure his dramatic unmaking before the public. He thus reflects: "The private pain I could have endured. But the deliberate public humiliation was too much for me" (xv). Yet, within an information society, the separation between the private and the public life (fundamental to the idea of the individual under modernity) becomes irrelevant. The circus at the warehouse demonstrates the degree to which a narrative of success is now a function of a media spectacle whose outcome seems decided *in advance*.

Iacocca is not an "advertisement for myself" but an "advertisement for my corporation." Corporate America works in tandem with Madison Avenue and Hollywood to manufacture a variety of images for the successful individual. Iacocca's eventual resurrection, like his fall, is a product of this combination. The connection between business enterprise and image culture is made manifest in the structure of the book, which is organized around the author's corporate image. The twenty-eight chapters are broken down into four sections. The two middle sections—"The Ford Story" and "The Chrysler Story"—carry the names of the two automobile manufacturers for whom Iacocca worked. The first and last sections—"Made in America" and "Straight Talk"—are advertising slogans made popular on radio and television in the early 1980s by Chrysler pitchman Lee Iacocca. The "Made in America" motto emerged in the early eighties as a part of Chrysler's campaign to sell nostalgia for the old-fashioned work ethic through the theme of "Yankee Ingenuity." Iacocca, in a television commercial aired during the summer of 1982, stated: "There was a time when 'Made in America' meant something. It meant you made the best. Unfortunately, a lot of Americans don't believe that anymore, and maybe with good reason. . . . We in the car industry must make 'Made in America' mean something again."[22] In response to the national crisis brought on by the globalization of the economy during the eighties (for U.S. automakers, this event was marked by American consumers' increased demand for European and especially Japanese cars), this ad illustrates an effort to renew faith in the Protestant ethos. If "Made in America" had once been a sign of quality products, it was now an ad slogan aimed at consumers.

The blockbuster sales of *Iacocca* illustrate a resurgence of national interest in the man who not only fulfilled the dream of success but had the capacity to "make 'Made in America' mean something again." The book simultaneously borrowed from the Chrysler advertising campaign and cashed in on the post–Civil Rights white ethnic craze. Unlike industrialist Andrew Carnegie, who enters a narrative of moral luck only after distancing himself from his immigrant father and swallowing his Scottish accent, Iacocca sells white ethnic nostalgia by highlighting his familial roots and his life as an "Italian Yankee" (37). His autobiography updates the traditional story of class mobility by generating a tale of American enterprise that emphasizes ethnic heritage over economic hardship. Iacocca concludes the book's Prologue with the sentence, "Now let me tell you my story" (xv), but opens the first chapter (titled "Family") with a tribute to his immigrant father. It begins: "Nicola Iacocca, my father, arrived in this country in 1902 at the age of twelve—poor, alone, and scared" (3). *Iacocca* thus starts not with Lido's birth but with the ordeals endured by his Italian father, Nicola, upon arrival in the New World. Nicola Iacocca is a Horatio Alger hero with an Italian accent. In Allentown, Pennsylvania, he "pursued the American dream with all his might . . . he was full of ambition and hope" (4–5). Self-employed, he saved his money and became the proprietor of local restaurants and movie houses.

For the son of Nicola, financial distress is overwritten by the experience of persistent ethnic prejudice in school and at work. Although Lido Iacocca did not rise from the immigrant ghetto,[23] neither is he Henry Ford II, the spoiled grandson of Henry Ford who sticks his silver foot in his mouth every time he makes a racist, anti-Semitic, or nativist remark. If Nicola is the immigrant-as-enterprising-man, his son is the second-generation ad man in the Anglocentric melting pot of corporate America. The latter's high school and college days teach him the importance of "luck" (21) and pluck. In the tradition of Ben Franklin, he maintains his self-discipline by keeping a daily "schedule" and weekly "outline" (20). In 1946, Lee Iacocca accepted his first job with Ford Motor Company. Imagining himself as the "Italian Yankee," he describes the personality-enhancing process by which he "made" himself into a skillful salesman (32). This explains why, as a seasoned businessman, he is a "great believer" in the Dale Carnegie Institute for self-improvement (54) and openly critical of the "faceless personality" management style at General Motors (58).

Prior to the 1970s, his experience in corporate culture taught him that there were definite limits to the uses of personality. Iacocca's first thirty years in marketing convinced him that "there were certain broad standards you just didn't violate": namely, a corporate chairman should never appear in his company's ads (268). Thus he acknowledges his skepticism when asked by Chrysler's ad agency, immediately after being hired as the company head in 1978, to appear in television commercials. If the idea of an inner character now seemed antiquated, the notion of the media-made personality was imminent. Like it or not, Iacocca became a recognizable face after the press attention he received during the 1979 congressional hearings, where Chrysler was awarded $1.5 billion in loan guarantees to avoid bankruptcy. Chrysler's ad agency, Kenyon and Eckhardt, exploited his celebrity status in a successful effort to reinvigorate the car company's image and thereby increase its products' market share. They did so by staging television and radio commercials in which Iacocca's expressive face and familiar voice made personal appeals and guarantees to the consumer on behalf of an otherwise impersonal and increasingly transnational corporation. The entrepreneur was now a media-manufactured commodity.

Iacocca was instantaneously transformed from salesman to celebrity. The press now courted him as a prospective presidential candidate. In the summer of 1982, he was featured in the middle of the front page of the *Wall Street Journal*, where "his cocksure personality" was offered as evidence that here was "the lone colorful auto man in a faceless sea." Responding to the media query, "If a Hollywood star can [become President], why not a Detroit car salesman?"[24] Iacocca reflects: "I guess the rumors started because of all the TV commercials I did for Chrysler. Many people now think I'm an actor. But that's ridiculous. Everybody knows that being an actor doesn't qualify you to be President!" (267). It is unclear whether Iacocca simply thinks that an actor is unqualified to be the nation's highest elected public official or whether he believes as well that it is "ridiculous" to assume that he is an actor. Obviously, neither was the case. In 1984, the president of the United States was a Hollywood actor and the country's most beloved entrepreneur was a celebrity. Media culture, in its capacity to collapse the distinctions between the private and public spheres and the inner and outer selves, also flattens the distinction between actors, entrepreneurs, and presidents.

Nowhere is this more evident than in Ross Perot's 1992 media-driven third-party candidate run for president of the United States, where the self-made billionaire posed before the American people as a charismatic populist folk hero. Such a farce compels us to update Iacocca's ironic proclamation by substituting "entrepreneur" for "actor." When, on 1 October 1992, Perot reentered the presidential race, he echoed Iacocca's sentiments from a decade past.[25] He told reporters and supporters that his decision to run was simple. "We must make the words 'Made in the U.S.A.' once again the world's standard for excellence," to which he added: "we've got to pass on the American dream to . . . our children and grandchildren." His personal stake in the American dream was succinctly summed up in a one-sentence Algeresque invocation of moral luck: "I have been extremely fortunate during my business career."

Rather than use the campaign platform to detail his own road to riches, Perot shifted focus from himself to the first-generation Jewish immigrant grandfather of Mort Myerson, president of Electronic Data Systems, a corporation owned by Perot from the early 1960s to the mid-1980s. With every bit as much courage and sacrifice as Nicola Iacocca, grandpa Myerson fled Russia "because he happened to be a Jew. He lived in an attic in Brooklyn for eighteen months working as a tailor . . . so he could get together the money to buy a train ticket to Fort Worth, Texas." On the day Myerson was promoted to president of EDS, his ninety-five-year-old grandfather, "with tears in his eyes," told his grandson: "through you I have fulfilled all of the dreams I had as a young man when I came to America." The elder Myerson, who escaped religious persecution in the Old World, realized his immigrant dream by means of hard work, decency and, belatedly, his grandson's achievements. Perot's elaborate and emotional story of grandpa Myerson stands in stark contrast to the brevity and restraint of his description of how, by being "extremely fortunate," he inherited the American dream. More than humility may be operating here, however. Perot's televised speech deflects detailed inquiries concerning how he built his financial empire, as well as allegations against him regarding anti-Semitism, through the strategic placement of an uplifting story about a turn-of-the-century immigrant.[26] His brief comment on his own self-made success is coded by white moral luck, a convention he used repeatedly in his two-part "Conversation with Ross Perot," the half-hour autobiographical infomercials aired on cable and network television just before the November elections.

Downsizing: Susan Powter and Oprah Winfrey

In an era of infomercials and the celebrity, narratives of self-made success foreground the body rather than the soul and, in doing so, collapse the distinctions between image and reality, private and public selves. Women's uplift stories often complicate this narrative transformation by representing the female body as an object to be scorned or desired and as an instrument for self-imprisonment or self-empowerment. Think only of enterprising entertainers like Madonna or Cher, who have maintained a certain amount of financial independence from men (husbands and lovers) throughout their careers. Each has shrewdly transformed her celebrity image not merely by changing the clothes she wears but by resculpting her figure through diet, exercise, and surgery. Even more than the contemporary self-made man, today's self-made woman is as likely to be as much a product of cosmetic surgery as a producer of cosmetics.

As previous chapters of this study indicate, over the past century enterprising women have been most successful in exploiting consumer society's desire to adorn the female form. Business pioneers such as Harriet Ayer and Madam Walker marketed fashion trends as a means of personal autonomy outside their marriages. However, today's enterprising woman sells her media-manufactured image—including her story of self-making—as the product of entrepreneurial triumph. If Emma McChesney made the pitch to the petticoat customer, "I not only sell it, I wear it," today's female celebrity might say to her customers, "I not only sell it, I am it." While she peddles an objectified self-image to her lusting (largely male) viewership, the successful woman offers her adoring (largely female) fans an enabling ideal for remaking themselves. The media-manufactured woman is neither wholly objectified nor simply empowered; as narratives of the female celebrity suggest, she is both simultaneously. Even as these women provide their fans with models for self-improvement and uplift, they belong to the multimillion-dollar-a-year diet, fitness, and medical establishment, which targets female consumers by promoting nearly impossible (if not unnatural or unhealthy) standards of beauty.

Perhaps no self-made woman in America fits this contradictory profile better than Australian-born fitness guru Susan Powter, host of the late-night infomercial "Stop the Insanity!" and author of the best-selling autobiographical book by the same name. The fact that Powter's infomercial and book share the same name demonstrates the extent to which, particularly within an image society, the individual sells the product. Whereas the traditional self-made man sold his story as an afterthought to the accumulation of riches, the celebrity's primary source of income is her story. *Celebrity is the self that sells.*

With the eclipse of the traditional, character-based entrepreneur by the media personality, the "self" has become more superficial but no less germane to American success.

Powter is the self-proclaimed "housewife who figured it out."[27] In infomercial and autobiography alike, she moves deftly from fitness guru to girlfriend. As she reminds her audience, she is an "expert by experience" (212). Born and raised in Sydney, Australia, she was educated at a Dominican convent school prior to accompanying her family to the United States at age ten. She dropped out of high school in the ninth grade, and worked as a nurse's aide and a secretary. Later, living in Texas, she met and married Prince Charming (which is how she refers to her first husband throughout *Stop the Insanity!*), the man of her dreams: "If not the American dream, the Cinderella one" (40). After six weeks of marriage, her doctor told her she was four weeks pregnant; her second child was conceived two months after the birth of her first. Although taught to believe that motherhood would be her "fulfillment" and drawing consolation from being anointed a saint by her husband's Catholic family, back-to-back births made Powter feel the loss of her sexuality, freedom, energy and, eventually, her marriage (43). In the meantime, the Prince demanded fulfillment of what Mary Antin once referred to as "our national ideal of manhood." Powter puts it this way: "One of the Prince's biggest worries, or insecurities, was his need to work for himself. To not be under anyone's thumb. To feel like a man" (47).

Powter not only performed the traditional tasks of the self-made man's wife, she updated the role for the 1980s. Caring for two infants and supporting her husband's entrepreneurial ambitions was not enough. She felt a need to look sexy while doing it. While the Prince assumed the role of the "young, good-looking entrepreneur," she desperately tried to get "skinny" in order to fulfill her duty as "his pink paisley wife." Soon the young wife not only realized that her "self-worth was second to his," but that her husband's business venture gave him "a sense of accomplishment that I was severely lacking." Moreover, while she stayed at home changing diapers and battling her weight, he found another way to validate his manhood: he engaged in extramarital affairs while running the family business. The unequal relationship between businessman and wife proved to be the unmaking of the Prince's and Powter's "entrepreneurial life together" (47–49).

For the author of *Stop the Insanity!*, the end of her American Cinderella dream is manifested through a complete loss of control over her body. As the "Prince's life grew: his business, his list of girlfriends," so did his ex-wife's body, which bloated to 260 pounds. Awakening one day from her "fat coma" (51), Powter says she "did what all of us have done. I went to the diet industry—the first biggest mistake of my life" (60). When dieting failed, she turned to the fitness industry and found an aerobic atmosphere rigged not only to ignore the needs of but also to humiliate overweight women. With two strikes against her, Powter chose her own way out: she simply "went for a walk."

> There wasn't a fitness goal or physical image in my mind. When I went for a walk I felt better, so I just took a walk. . . . I wanted to walk forever. Walk away from my life and into someone else's, preferably that of a beautiful model, a successful businesswoman, or one of those women who have children and still fit into their "old high school jeans." (78–79)

Inasmuch as walking involves continuous movement and breathing, this simple act (along with eating high-volume, low-fat foods) became the cornerstone of Powter's "wellness" program. Even as the author rejects the diet industry's unhealthy prescriptions for weight loss and the fitness industry's unreasonable workout regimes, she nonetheless advocates many of the standards of beauty promoted by them. This is made evident in Powter's autobiography by the slippage between actual fitness and the image of fitness. The self-image she promotes as "strong, lean, and healthy" includes not only exercise (for good health) but cosmetic surgery (for good looks). By simultaneously repudiating the means by which corporate America promotes femininity and embracing its ends, Powter speaks to the contradictory desires of large numbers of women. Even as they search for commonsense alternatives, they still want to become the diet industry's ideal type. Powter is a charismatic ideal for her female audience:

the self-made woman who not only owns her own line of designer clothes but has overcome the struggle to fit into them. Her viewers shed the limitations of their own lives and identify with the successful and entertaining self-image projected by their infomercial host.

Powter has built her career by both terrorizing and profiting from the diet and fitness industries. Prodding her largely female readership to "hear your own story mixed in with mine" (15), her popular authority derives from her capacity to speak directly to the desires and real-life experiences of ordinary women. Powter's narrative weds her life story to good business sense in order to demonstrate the health dangers of a profit-driven diet industry. Early in the book, for example, she cites well-known studies that reveal the high percentage of teenage girls on weight-loss diets. So as to humanize the cold statistics, Powter offers a personal anecdote—dubbed the "cider vinegar story"—to illustrate her own teenage insanity. At age thirteen, the author says she tried just about anything to lose weight, even a combination diet of kelp, lecithin capsules, and cider vinegar. Around the same time, her family noticed that her two-year-old brother, whenever in the presence of his older sister, had the habit of squinching his nose and mumbling something akin to "P U—dirty socks!" In hindsight, Powter realizes that "the cider vinegar was oozing from every pore in my body, and I smelled like . . . dirty socks" (29). Although this weight-loss story is amusing, it makes the point that methods for achieving the ideal self-image can be hazardous to your health. It can also be expensive, as she explains on the next page. She instructs her reader on the "insanity" of blindly following the prescriptions of the diet industry:

> Think about this. Business 101. You give "them" your hard-earned money. Then they tell you what kind of starvation you'll be living on. . . . Business 101 tells me that if I pay you for a temporary, painful—and dieting is painful—solution to my problem, if the solution I am paying for will absolutely set me up for failure, and if I will need you again in a couple of months, then this is not . . . a good investment. (30)

In a book "for women, about women getting well" (13) and looking good, Powter deploys the language of entrepreneurship to assess the diet industry's bottom line. As she states with characteristic bluntness, "manufacturers [of diet products] lie for profit" (110).

Whether pitching her "wellness" program in *Stop the Insanity!* or discussing teen pregnancies on her nationally syndicated talk show, Powter sells her licensed products to her largely female viewership by shifting from fitness expert to next-door neighbor. In this sense, she is a product of the Oprahfication of the television talk-show format,[28] where the audience identifies not merely with the program's guests (as on *Oprah's* forerunner, the *Phil Donahue Show*) but with the host. In turn, the distinction between guest and host disappears as the audience absorbs frequent personal confessions from the talk-show host. The once plump Oprah made her national reputation—in her 1985 screen debut in *The Color Purple* and on her talk show, which began airing nationwide a year later—by being opinionated but nurturing. Media critics began describing her in terms of the black mammy stereotype: "nearly 200 pounds of Mississippi-bred black womanhood, brassy, earthy, street smart and soulful," retorted the first national news story to profile Winfrey's talk-showmanship.[29] The hard-bodied Powter, by contrast, who sports spiky bleached-blonde hair above Vulcan-like ears, is a friendly but firm alien-outsider from Down Under. Although both Oprah and Powter are exotic enough to pique the curiosity of their middle-American TV viewership,[30] they are domesticated enough to be invited back into their living rooms on a regular basis. Television brings the world into the home and offers viewers what Jean Baudrillard characterizes as an "ecstasy of communication."[31] By collapsing inside (home) and outside (world), foreground (self) and background (scene), TV allows viewers to inhabit the space of audience and celebrity simultaneously.

It is not unimportant that Powter's major moneymakers—her fitness video *Lean, Strong, and Healthy* as well as *Stop the Insanity!*—appeared around the same time as *Oprah's* 1993 "Weight Loss Show," which detailed the host's life-defining battle with weight loss. As early as the national debut of the *Oprah Winfrey Show* in September 1986, the host confided to her viewers: "I don't have a lot of problems in my life. . . . But two things have bugged me for years. The first, my thighs. The second, my love life."[32] Winfrey's bootstrap story would do Madam Walker proud. She was born into poverty on a small farm in Mississippi and later reared in the inner city of Milwaukee before becoming a TV personality and media mogul. However, her repeated attempts to adhere to conventional standards of femininity through dieting and dating dampened her personal evaluation of her own success. Oprah appeared to have cleared the first of these last two hurdles by the end of 1988. On November 15 of that year, she taped her now-famous "Diet Show." Before a live audience, the host stripped off her jacket to reveal a svelte figure squeezed into a pair of size ten Calvin Klein jeans. To demonstrate her newfound control over her never-ending struggle with weight, the 145-pound Oprah paraded around the stage in her Calvin's with a little red wagon. The kiddy toy hauled sixty-seven pounds of beef fat, or precisely the amount the host had shed through a severe eighteen-week, four-hundred-calories-a-day liquid diet program. When the show aired three days later, it won a 16.4 rating—equivalent to a remarkable 45 percent share of the U.S. television market—making *Oprah* the highest-rated talk show in syndication.[33]

Within a year, Oprah gained back the weight she had lost. Given that 98 percent of all diets end in failure, this comes as no surprise. What shocked her adoring fans was a disclosure regarding the cover of the 20 August–1 September 1989 issue of *TV Guide*, which pictured Oprah Winfrey. An apparent photo of the sexy, sequin-clad millionaire perched atop a pile of money next to the headline "Oprah! The Richest Woman on TV" was revealed to be a morphed image of Oprah's head onto Ann-Margret's colorized body. Over the past decade, in scattered responses to questions about how it feels to have accumulated such a fortune, Oprah claims that her entrepreneurial acumen has a "deep spiritual" meaning: "It's symbolic of what I am supposed to do in my life."[34] Her beliefs are expressed in terms commonly associated with New Age religion, specifically its concept of "prosperity consciousness." This philosophy explains her rise from poverty to prosperity as a sign of a higher calling. It emphasizes not only the individual's responsibility for amassing wealth. The alteration of self-image is a prerequisite to ascending the ladder of success. In this light, New Age prosperity consciousness can be seen as a spiritual addendum to New Thought, whose maxim was "think and grow rich."[35] Yet, as the Oprah Winfrey–Ann-Margret composite on the cover of *TV Guide* illustrates, the news and entertainment industry tends to look elsewhere when marketing the celebrity's self-made fortune. Simply put, the mass media privileges body-image over self-awareness when presenting the story of Oprah's uplift to the public at large.

It may seem absurd to measure people's professional accomplishments according to their capacity to lose weight or look sexy. Yet even Oprah publicly acknowledged (by airing parts of her private diary on her November 1993 "Weight Loss Show," and more recently, by publishing these revelations as a part of her autobiographical sketch titled "Oprah's Story")[36] that her physical self-image became the standard she employed to assess her success. In a journal entry dated 13 December 1989, she wrote: "The new studio is looking great. . . . The farmhouse is coming together too. So why do I feel compelled to eat?" An entry for 20 February 1991 reads: "gained eight pounds, bringing me to an all-time whopping 226 pounds. . . . I don't know this self. . . . I caught a glimpse of myself reflected in a store window. I didn't recognize the fat lady staring back at me." The misrecognition suggests the manner in which the feminine self—here mirrored in a mall window—is preceded by images of beauty thrown up by consumer culture. The advertised image, such as Ann-Margret's body, becomes the measure of real-life womanhood. Another year passed before Oprah began the painful process of realigning her corpulent self with the feminine ideal through weight-loss instruction that combined more sensible eating with rigorous exercise. The occasion for making public the diary entries, *Oprah*'s "Weight Loss Show," opened with the host's confession: "I've kept journals almost all my life. And although I've experienced some incredible changes throughout my career, my weight was all-consuming."

Today's self-made woman is not only required to make money but—in order to be perceived as in control and therefore successful—must look good while making it. This explains why Oprah was consumed by her failure to control her self-image, which seemed to overshadow her achievements as a media mogul. This also elucidates

119

the logic behind Susan Powter's revision of Sophie Tucker's aphorism, "I've been rich and I've been poor, and rich is better," with "I've been fit and I've been fat, and fit is better" (18). For Powter, reconstructing the body precedes not only emotional sanity but financial prowess as well. Powter's anti-New Thought success motto identifies the problem in the simplest terms: "It's not in your mind, it's in your body."

If *Stop the Insanity!* has one goal it is this: "change your body forever" (102). However, while good fitness might generate the conditions under which the enterprising individual can scale the mountain to success, more important in today's image-generated culture is simply looking good—too often regardless of health hazards. Cosmetic surgery is to the celebrity what steroids have become to the bodybuilder. Despite her emphasis on good health, Susan Powter uses the word "superficial" to introduce one of her more salient personality traits (15). In the course of her book, she advocates cosmetic surgery for all those who want to look as well as feel fit, and then confesses to having had a tummy tuck and an ear job (276–77). The superficial nature of celebritydom suggests the distance between it and, say, the inner soul in an age of character, or even willpower in the high era of personality. In a recent interview, Powter clarified her intent: "The message is: you make your own money, and here's how to do it. First, have the energy to get out of bed."[37] Powter's prescription does not revisit the modern debate about entrepreneurial uplift: character versus personality. Instead, it displaces the opposition altogether. As she instructs her students: "The problem is not your lack of mind power, discipline, self-control, or 'eating disorder.' . . . It's not in your mind, it's in your body" (87). Or, as she plainly put it in an interview with the *New York Times Magazine*, "The most empowering thing is to be physically well."[38]

Powter's turning point occurred while shopping—what she calls her "moment in the mall" (85). Inverting Oprah's painful moment of misrecognition in the store window, Powter first recognized the reality of her new, downsized self-image when, while strolling in a local mall, she realized that her thighs no longer rubbed together. The euphoria helped propel her on her way toward entrepreneurial uplift.

However, Powter, like nonconventional self-made individuals before her, insists that "luck" had "nothing to do" with her mercurial rise. For women raised on romantic fairy tales, she maintains: "There was no magical moment. . . . the fairy godmother is a lie" (78). Powter insists that hard work coupled with common sense has allowed her to become the superwoman of her post-Cinderella dreams. In fact, she is a mom who models her line of designer clothing as a part of her larger success. Nonetheless, her book demonstrates the extent to which the new media age has not brought with it an end to the enterprising woman's need to negotiate her gender identity. In order to combat certain protocols of femininity and look good while doing it, Powter advocates a high-heeled form of feminist critique. *Stop the Insanity!* reveals not only the author's love of pumps but, as will become apparent, the literal and symbolic role high heels play in her professional downfall as well as her entrepreneurial climb.

Powter takes a high-heeled feminist approach to her fat-to-fit-to-famous story in a chapter titled "Life Changes." It opens with a photo of the author in a confident if sexy pose, donning her trademark buzz cut, and wearing nothing more than a thong bikini and high heels (280). It is, we learn later, one of her favorite likenesses, "much closer to the truth" (322) of who she really is than other professional portraits in circulation. The image sets the tone for the entire chapter, which describes Powter's literal and figurative fall prior to her entrepreneurial ascent. When her ex-husband failed to make regular alimony and child-support payments, Powter supplemented her income by holding jobs in a variety of traditional female occupations, including two stay-at-home jobs (babysitter and cooking instructor) and a stint as a secretary. None of these satisfied her emotional or economic need for independence. "It was time to decide how I was going to make a living and not compromise what was important to me. I got fit, then changed my body and started feeling and looking better, and establishing some sanity in my life" (298). Rather than establish psychological stability prior to making changes in other facets of her life, Powter made a change in her physical well-being: she "got fit." After transforming her self-image "from a 260-pound housewife to a lean machine" (308), she made a career decision that "many of you may regard as insane." She put her new body to work in a strip club. "I had just lived through the inequality in women's lives. The Prince's rules were different from mine. I looked at the system and figured if that's the way it is, I'll not only join them—I'll beat them at their own game." Powter attempts to slip the corset of women's "inequality"—from feminine ideals to women's work—by seizing these constraints and turning them into a means of economic independence. Employing a pseudonym and otherwise disguised by little else than a wig, a G-string, and high heels, Powter finally moves out from underneath the authority of her ex-husband by dancing for dollars. "I knew if I was ever going to pull myself up by those damn bootstraps that everyone was telling me about, I'd need money. . . . I wanted a job that required no commitment and very little time, that gave me hours that worked for me and the children and lots of cash" (298).

If, as Powter claims, topless dancing became the first step toward "rebuilding my financial future" (300), it also proved to be something of a misstep. Powter avoids romanticizing this period of her life because, upon reflection, she recognizes the extent to which exotic dancing is not so far from other female jobs she previously performed, such as being a housewife or a secretary: "I see topless dancing as a very honest example of what life is really like for most women. We parade our wares in front of all the men, they ogle and admire and pay cash, they pick the one they want, and we walk away thinking we have security" (301). Powter takes this credo to its logical conclusion when she turns from dancing to sex for money; or, in her words, "a socially acceptable form of prostitution." After being introduced to a wealthy customer at her strip club, she begins an intimate affair with him: "We dated and slept together, and he gave me cash. That's what it was, and never—not for a second—did I think it was anything else" (304).

Given that self-making within an electronic media culture is realized along the surface of the body rather through the cultivation of character, stripping and prostitution have perhaps become more permissible forms of enterprise. Powter's turn to prostitution might thus be read as a literal gloss on Christopher Lasch's figure of the "happy hooker," who, the author of *The Culture of Narcissism* sardonically claimed, today "stands in place of Horatio Alger as the prototype of personal success."[39] Powter is, no doubt, more Moll Flanders than Robinson Crusoe. But in the tradition of her literary foremother, prostitution afforded Powter a certain degree of economic stability and personal autonomy. Specifically, an illicit relationship with a wealthy, married man enabled her to pursue a career in fitness. Free from the grind of exotic dancing, she could afford to be poorly paid as an entry-level aerobic instructor. Teaching up to five fitness classes a day was not simply a lesson in the Protestant work ethic but offered Powter her first taste of professional fulfillment. However, prostitution—the very thing that provided her a means toward taking her first step up the ladder of success—brought with it a dogged sense of self-exploitation that dampened her newfound self-worth. Feeling "strangled," she abandoned the sex-for-cash arrangement. With nowhere else to go, she returned to exotic dancing, hoping that she could continue teaching aerobics in the daytime. Her retreat to the strip club stage lasted only one night. During the final set of her first night back, Powter, elevated by stiletto pumps, slipped on a customer's spilled beer and "flipped" off the stage: "When I say flipped, I mean I did a complete flip and landed in five-inch heels on both feet" (306). The fall resulted in severely broken feet but also turned out to be the last obstacle in Powter's road to riches. Confined to a wheelchair for months, she realized her professional calling: sharing with others the idea that fitness is for everyone.

Here, a gap appears in *Stop the Insanity!*, one that corresponds to the three years prior to the release of the book. Although Powter immediately informs us that she found her vocation—"change the face of fitness"—she leaves unsaid just how, during the first years of the 1990s, she financed her fitness scheme. Of course, the nuts and bolts of business decisions have never been a staple of narratives of the self-made man, which operate through familiar if formulaic tropes (e.g., luck and pluck; timetables) rather than the details of day-to-day business operations. Nevertheless, the reader never learns how she financed her fitness empire. The silence is, in part, a symptom of Powter's gendered narrative, which, as Emma McChesney finally conceded, compels the author of *Stop the Insanity!* to give more weight to personal affairs than corporate ones. Specifically, Powter sidetracks her entrepreneurial adventures with inside information about her romance with her soon-to-be second husband. Advice about business aptitude is reduced to her trademark message: a fit body is the foundation of healthy finances. "That's what changing my body has meant to me," Powter concludes toward the end of the "Life Changes" chapter. "Yeah, it's cool that I do national TV, write books, do seminars, and own and operate a very successful business, but it's even cooler that I'm in control and have choices now" (318).

As it turns out, Powter had less dominion over her fitness empire than she let on. About a year after the publication of *Stop the Insanity!*, she publicly complained about the lack of control she exercised over the Susan Powter Corporation, which was estimated to have sales of more than $50 million. She began suing for control of the company. She alleged to have been coerced into signing a contract that gave two Dallas investors, brothers Gerald and Richard Frankel, 50 percent of her business and left her cash poor and owing creditors $3.2 million. Three months later, in January 1995, she filed for bankruptcy, claiming that legal fees had wiped her out.[40] "Here I am," Powter fumed to a reporter, "the only revenue generator, writing, producing, talking, selling, doing seminars, telling *my* story, for God's sake, and they decided it was theirs to market as they please."[41] Rather than blemish the profitable image of self-made success surrounding his corporation's namesake, Gerald Frankel used the rags-to-riches story to counter her testimony: "The year before we formed our partnership, she made $14,000 a year as an aerobics instructor. . . . We put close to $1 million into an absolutely unknown, and over the next two years [she] made over $3 million."[42]

As Powter says, "my story" is what is at stake here. In an age of celebrity, the entrepreneur's uplift saga is not intended simply to be put in the service of maintaining a form of America's national identity. The story itself has become the individual's way to wealth. After all, what else is celebrity but the commodification of the self? If, after the death of the self-made man, the figure of success has been recycled, it seems only logical that she would become the product of an electronic society. In a world increasingly dominated by mass media, the distinction between actual self and self-image (in narratives of self-making as elsewhere) has collapsed.

Susan Powter's post–*Stop the Insanity!* saga points to the limited authority successful individuals have over the circulation of their stories in era in which a shrinking number of media conglomerates control public access to information. Take the example of Powter's attempt to compete directly with *Oprah* by moving from the 2 A.M. infomercial format to daytime talk-show television. At the outset, the host of the *Susan Powter Show* (which first aired in the fall of 1994) had some very clear ideas about what the show would and would not be. "There will be no tabloid issues at all," she told a *Los Angeles Times* reporter. "There's no exploiting people at all. . . . and if that doesn't fly on TV, it ain't gonna fly."[43] The show ran in two hundred markets for more than a year before being pulled off the air because of low ratings. Powter blames television executives, who were unable to see beyond a tabloid format, for failing to fulfill her vision: "It started to be about real conversation, but the producers turned it into a tabloid—'Teens from Hell' and 'Why Doesn't He Love Me Anymore?'"[44]

Despite her efforts to maintain a certain degree of respectability on her TV show, Powter is a product of tabloid culture, which can make and unmake her success story. The mass media is increasingly saturated by a tabloid sensibility that fixates on the sensational and the scandalous while eroding the distinction between fact and fiction, truth and lie. When, in the Afterword to *Stop the Insanity!* (titled "Tabloid 101"), Powter defends herself against allegations made on tabloid TV's *Inside Edition* that she never weighed 260 pounds, she does less to discredit the hoax than reinforce the reader's perception of her as a media personality. Despite Powter's predictable complaints about tabloid journalism, *Stop the Insanity!* is littered with favorable references to the same. Throughout the book, she conveys the authenticity of her personal experiences (love and marriage [41], her ex-husband's extramarital affairs [46], prostitution [304]) through explicit references to tabloid magazines and television (*Cosmo*, *Donahue*, and *Geraldo*, respectively). At the end of the book's Introduction, Powter describes a flight to Los Angeles, during which she had her first face-to-face encounter with Dolly Parton, who also had recently gone through a much-publicized period of downsizing. The anecdote is paradigmatic for how the self-referential signs of uplift operate in today's consumer society:

> Dolly Parton is my idol. My nails need just a bit more acrylic, and the high heels, I've got them down (see my "after" picture). I'll never be able to match the big hair, but let me strive. Strive to be Dolly.
>
> During our flight a couple of people asked Dolly for her autograph. She was so polite, accommodating and sweet, but what was going on two seats behind her was blowing my mind. At least sixteen people came up to me asking questions, wanting an autograph, or just telling me that they were eating, breathing, and moving, and their lives were changing. (19)

In her story about meeting Dolly, Powter transgresses the border between "before" (a star-crossed fan) and "after" (a star who, apparently, is bigger than her idol).

In media culture, where the distance between the actual reality and advertised image has eroded, the consumer's desire "to be" an idol of success is potentially fulfilled by mirroring the charismatic face on the cover of a tabloid magazine or by becoming the sexy figure on the TV screen. This explains Powter's parenthetical aside ("see my 'after' picture"), which refers to the trademark hard-bodied, high-heeled swimsuit photograph mentioned earlier. At the start of her first fitness video, *Lean, Strong, and Healthy*, Powter, clad in a workout leotard, stands between life-size "before" (fat and slovenly) and "after" (fit and sexy) images of herself. Yet, the leotard-clad host looks as little like her "after" portrait as her "before" photo.[45] The staging of the opening video shot illustrates the workings of self-making within image society: the firm but friendly host inspires her audience to follow her instruction by leaving behind the ("before") self we are and by becoming the ("after") self we desire to be.

Epilogue: The Return of
the Self-Made Man

Although physical fitness has been an occasional ingredient in self-improvement recipes over the past century, it was not until the advent of media culture that it took hold as an integral part of narratives of self-making. Postmodern society—with its focus on depthless image instead of internal reality, celebrity rather than character—found a vehicle for marketing the idea of success in enterprising stories that foregrounded bodily transformations. Is it any wonder, then, that Arnold Schwarzenegger was at the forefront of the self-made man's rehabilitation? At the opening of *Arnold: The Education of a Body-builder*, the immigrant from Graz insists: "I *knew* I was going to be a bodybuilder. . . . I would be the best bodybuilder in the world, the greatest, the best-built man."[1] Unable to speak more than a few words of English when he first stepped onto U.S. shores in 1968, Schwarzenegger was already an American dreamer: "From the age of ten, I wanted to be the best. I thought I had been born in the wrong country. All I wanted to do was leave Austria and come to America. And when I got here I would not be one of the masses."[2] Prior to coming to America, young Arnold was a voracious reader of U.S. magazines such as *Muscle Builder* and *Mr. America,* which, he recalls, were "full of success stories" about bodybuilders turned movie stars. This, too, was Schwarzenegger's youthful ambition. From the start he understood that "bodybuilding was show business . . . [thus] I had to become a showman" (58). The image-making factories in Hollywood seemed a natural extension of the muscle pit, the big screen another form of exhibiting the exaggerated self before an audience.

The entertainment industry helped make Schwarzenegger not just a media celebrity but one of the richest men in the nation. For years Hollywood scripted his successive remakings for popular consumption. Moviegoers, most of whom were introduced to Schwarzenegger in the documentary *Pumping Iron* (1977), watched his transformation between the Reagan and Bush presidencies. With the help of films such as *Twins* (1988) and *Kindergarten Cop* (1990), his on-screen personality went from menacing muscle-bound/cyborgian alien in *The Terminator* (1984) to benevolent muscle-bound/cyborgian hero in its Spielbergian sequel, *Terminator 2: Judgment Day* (1992). Critics of the latter movie identified the kinder and gentler Schwarzenegger, who kneecaps rather than kills his enemies, as a metaphor for the United States' surgical bombing of Baghdad during the 1991 Gulf War. In the spirit of compassion, he delivers the following line in *Terminator 2* with his trademark foreign accent: "The more contact I have with humans, the more I can learn." The touching moment, as J. Hoberman suggests, perhaps marks the Americanization of the Arnold.[3] A few years back, Schwarzenegger's marriage to news personality and JFK niece Maria Shriver helped legitimate his claim to U.S. citizenship, which was officially obtained in 1983. With his appointment as chairman of President Bush's Council on Physical Fitness and Sports, the enterprising bodybuilder had climbed out of the local muscle pit and into the White House gym.

As promoter Ben Weider, dubbed the Napoléon of his sport, has been known to say, "Bodybuilding is important for nation building." Schwarzenegger carries the additional weight of being identified as the *Übermensch*, a label no doubt fueled by reports of his father's membership in the Nazi party. However, after the fall of the Third Reich, it is no longer acceptable (as it was in America of the 1920s) to promote oneself as a Nordic self-made man. By maintaining his Germanic name and accent, however, the individual once known as the Austrian Oak proudly claims a white ethnic identity suitable to the post–Civil Rights Era in America. In a sense, he is the opposite side of the same coin that bears the visage of Clarence Thomas. Whereas whiteness, for Schwarzenegger, is that which need not speak its name but which is imaged in conspicuous ways, blackness, for Thomas, is that which must be disclaimed in the name of merit-based achievement. These proverbial twins, taken together, illustrate the maintenance of racial difference in representations of self-made success, where blackness is negated and whiteness is unmarked as the norm.

In the well-worn tradition of the self-made man in America, Schwarzenegger uses his capacity for order and self-discipline in his rise to the top. "The meaning of life," he meditates in *Arnold*, "is not simply to exist, to survive, but to move ahead, to go up, to achieve, to conquer" (112). The "secret" to his success is a "three-part formula"— "self-confidence, a positive mental attitude, and honest hard work" (30)—which is developed through his daily workout but implicitly inspired by the legacy of New Thought. If moral luck is absent from this formula, then so is divine intervention. Although raised Catholic, one of the first lessons Schwarzenegger learns in the gym is that the individual alone is responsible for his self-making or unmaking: "if I achieved something in life, I shouldn't thank God for it, I should thank myself. It was the same thing if something bad happened. . . . if I wanted a great body, I had to build it. Nobody else could. Least of all God" (32). Rather than wait for good fortune to smile on him, he masters the art of self-improvement by studying his physique in minute detail:

> I discovered that taking measurements gave me both satisfaction and incentive. I measured my calves, arms and thighs regularly, and I'd be turned on if I saw I'd increased an eighth-inch or a half-inch. On a calendar I kept even fractional changes in measurements and weight. I had a photographer take pictures at least once a month. I studied each shot with a magnifying glass. (64)

Self-surveillance is not only the key to remaking the self in the sport of bodybuilding; it also provides voyeuristic pleasure ("I'd be turned on if I saw . . ."). Detailed knowledge of the self is provided by calendars and clocks, rulers and tape measures, photographic images and mirrors. Twenty-four hours a day, seven days a week, Schwarzenegger consults "lists and charts" (71). "My body has become like . . . a special clock," he observes, "that is tuned so well it only goes wrong one second in five years" (110). He also generates self-knowledge through a five-point list, which includes: checking his body chemistry, making the most of his strict parental upbringing, avoiding distractions, cultivating a positive attitude, and being open to self-criticism. "I went down this list periodically," he explains with a Franklinesque flourish, "and checked it off item by item" (66). For the reader who intends to imitate Arnold's success, the second part of "the education of a bodybuilder" is devoted to a detailed catalog of schedules and lists that inventory weight training, cardiovascular exercise, diet, and positive thinking.

From the moment Schwarzenegger entered the United States, he worked to fulfill what he calls his "master plan."[4] A five-time Mr. Universe and seven-time Mr. Olympia, Schwarzenegger instructs his readers that bodybuilding is not an end in itself but a means toward greater achievement: "If I had been able to change my body that much, I could also, through the same discipline and determination, change anything else I wanted" (28). Schwarzenegger makes bodybuilding a metaphor for pursuing entrepreneurial ambition in America. In the postmodern world, the ability to remake one's body offers an immediate, if somewhat superficial and nostalgic, gratification of the desire for self-creation. In our body-obsessed society, there may be a peculiar Horatio Alger appeal to the twenty-two-inch ballooned bicep. "People aren't *born* with arms like that, they make them," remarks George Butler, producer and director of *Pumping Iron*, which launched Schwarzenegger's movie career.[5] Yet, since the Arnold entered the world of bodybuilding in the late 1960s, the sport has become as much a product of synthetic drugs and cybertechnologies as it is a resistance to the condition of postmodernity. Today, body sculptors can do without anabolic steroids and plastic surgery no less than discipline and determination.

If bodybuilding has somehow come to signify entrepreneurial uplift, it can also act as a cautionary tale. Over an extended period of time, the toll taken by steroids on the body-in-training can be as menacing yet undetectable as the damage to the environment caused by a toxic spill. Bodybuilder Steve Michalik, winner of the 1975 Mr.

Universe and the consensus pick among his peers to end Schwarz-enegger's reign as Mr. Olympia, pumped himself full of steroids to the point of ruining his immune system. When Michalik was on the verge of being named the best-built man on earth, he was also in the initial stages of a drawn-out period of personal destruction. A self-made carcass, he could barely climb onto the stage at the 1975 Mr. Universe show: "I had a cholesterol level of over 400, my blood pressure was 240 over 110—but, Jesus Christ, I was a great-looking corpse," Michalik told journalist Paul Solotaroff. "No one had ever seen anything like me. . . . I had absolutely *perfect* symmetry: 19-inch arms, 19-inch calves, and a 54-inch chest that was exactly twice the size of my thighs. The crowd went bazongo, the judges all loved me." For Michalik, however, all sense of achievement was wiped out by the side effects of being juiced up on steroids: "The only feeling I was capable of anymore was deep, deep hatred."[6]

In 1983, after a decade of accumulating toxins, Michalik's body nearly ceased to function. Although he had experienced internal and external hemorrhaging for years, only now—when his muscles turned to jelly—did his darkest nightmare become reality. As Solotaroff describes it: "No matter how he worked them or what he shot into them, they lost their gleaming, osmotic hardness, and began to pooch out like $20 whitewalls."[7] Michalik somehow lasted a few more years on the tour, but by the fall of 1986, his internal organs were in a critical phase of meltdown. "I knew it was all over for me," Michalik confesses. "Every system in my body was shot, my testicles had shrunk to the size of cocktail peanuts." After years of abusing his body in the name of superficial self-improvement, "it was like, suddenly, all the bills were coming in."[8] Miraculously, he survived a stint in intensive care, but his once buffed body rapidly lost its luster and decomposed. Minus his daily diet of five pounds of chicken and a fistful of steroids, he dropped more than a hundred pounds in three weeks. Months later he entered a rigorous detox program. The one-time Mr. Universe "could scarcely jog around the block that first day," reports Solotaroff, "but in the sauna, it all started coming out of him: a viscous, green paste that oozed out of his eyes and nostrils."[9]

Finally, Michalik's body began purging the toxins that, ingested in order to build the perfect body, had all but ended his life.

Schwarzenegger and his public relations people, in the venerable tradition of the self-made man, are careful to avoid all mention of the darker sides to his own uplifting past, including his use of steroids during the 1970s. Instead, he upholds bodybuilding as a model for entrepreneurship by keeping his focus and ours on the bottom line: "It feels good being the best-built man in the world," he states matter-of-factly in *Arnold*, "but the question always comes up: Okay, how can you use that to make money?" (107). As a sport that literalizes self-making along the body's surface, bodybuilding is marketed to consumers for its promise to return a sense of power and control to the individual. Placing a nonconventional story of uplift, such as Steve Michalik's, alongside a highly publicized one like Arnold Schwarzenegger's compels us to ask: Which body is postmodern America?

We should not confuse our era with the Gilded Age, when captains of industry were revered as self-made men. In an image society, it is entertainers in the film, television, and music industries, such as Arnold Schwarzenegger, Oprah Winfrey, and Madonna, who capture the public's imagination. Today's self-made man is a recycled image, a commodity in search of an audience. The manufacture of self-styled success in the form of the celebrity forecloses the central concern behind old-fashioned narratives of uplift: the cultivation of inner morality made manifest in the character of the entrepreneur. How do we account, then, for the fact that in the past few years there has been a proliferation of interest in and discussion about restoring character-based morality to politics, education, and the family, as well as to corporate enterprise? It is, I think, misleading to interpret this development as a harbinger of the return of traditional virtue. Rather, calls for the restoration of character and morality are symptomatic of a national crisis over their disappearance.

Many people will no doubt continue to yearn for a time when the morality of success was integral to the nation's creed. Such nostalgia does little to address the cultural logic of our time, which does not prescribe immorality so much as refuse the distinction between morality and immorality altogether. This study addresses the political stakes associated with the collapse of that distinction inasmuch as it answers the question: Why did the traditional figure of the self-made man meet its end? The post–World War II corporate consolidation of the electronic media and the rise of the celebrity are only part of a longer story. At the beginning of this century, despite the best intentions of Progressive Era reformers, the Horatio Alger formula for success failed to survive its appropriation by women, blacks, and immigrants. This was not because these new faces of enterprise inherently lacked the qualities of character. Instead, their stories speak what the logic of personal uplift does not allow to be spoken: the separation of gendered spheres, racial segregation, and nativism on which the rags-to-respectability-and-riches model was based. In doing so, they expose morality as a discourse traditionally placed in the service of normative power.

Notes

Introduction

1. Irvin G. Wyllie, *The Self-Made Man in America: The Myth of Rags to Riches* (New Brunswick, N.J.: Rutgers University Press, 1954); John G. Cawelti, *Apostles of the Self-Made Man* (Chicago: University of Chicago Press, 1965). Aside from the books by Wyllie and Cawelti, there was a flurry of published studies on the American success creed during the third quarter of this century. They include Kenneth S. Lynn, *The Dream of Success: A Study of the Modern American Imagination* (Boston: Little, Brown, 1955); Richard Weiss, *The American Myth of Success: From Horatio Alger to Norman Vincent Peale* (New York: Basic Books, 1969); Richard M. Huber, *The American Idea of Success* (New York: McGraw-Hill, 1971); Lawrence Chenoweth, *The American Dream of Success: The Search for the Self in the Twentieth Century* (North Scituate, Mass.: Duxbury Press, 1974); Rex Burns, *Success in America: The Yeoman Dream and the Industrial Revolution* (Amherst: University of Massachusetts Press, 1976).

2. By using the concept of narrative rather than myth in my study, I try to avoid some of the methodological pitfalls of traditional American Studies scholarship, commonly known as the "myth and symbol" school of criticism. The inaugural work in this influential tradition is Henry Nash Smith's *Virgin Land: The American West as Symbol and Myth* (Cambridge: Harvard University Press, 1950). For a brief overview of the "myth and symbol" school, see Myra Jehlen, "Introduction: Beyond Transcendence," in *Ideology and Classic American Literature*, ed. Sacvan Bercovitch and Myra Jehlen (New York: Cambridge University Press, 1986), 2–4.

3. Toni Morrison, "Unspeakable Things Unspoken: The Afro-American Presence in American Literature," *Michigan Quarterly Review* 28 (winter 1989): 13.

4. "Bush Announces the Nomination of Thomas to Supreme Court," *Congressional Quarterly Weekly Report* 49 (6 July 1991): 1851.

5. Robert J. Dole, quoted in John E. Yang and Sharon LaFraniere, "Bush Picks Thomas for Supreme Court," *Washington Post*, 2 July 1991, A1.

6. Clarence Thomas, letter to the editor, *Wall Street Journal*, 20 February 1987, 21.

7. Clarence Thomas's statement before the conference of black conservatives is quoted in Karen Tumulty, "Sister of High Court Nominee Traveled Different Road," *Los Angeles Times*, 5 July 1991, A4.

8. Emma Mae Martin's story was initially uncovered by Tumulty in "Sister of High Court Nominee Traveled Different Road." For further details, see Lisa Jones, "Invisible Ones," *Village Voice* 36 (12 November 1991), 27–28.

9. Emma Mae Martin, quoted in Tumulty, "Sister of High Court Nominee Traveled Different Road," A4.

10. Michel Foucault makes this point most succinctly in the first volume of *The History of Sexuality*, trans. Robert Hurley (New York: Vintage, 1980), 61–62.

11. Raymond Williams, *Keywords*, rev. ed. (London: Flamingo, 1983), 161–65.

12. Michel Foucault, *The Order of Things: An Archaeology of the Human Sciences* (New York: Vintage, 1973), 312.

13. Benjamin Franklin, *Autobiography*, ed. J. A. Leo Lemay and P. M. Zall (New York: Norton, 1986), 66, 70, 72.

14. Michel Foucault, *Discipline and Punish: The Birth of the Prison*, trans. Alan Sheridan (New York: Vintage, 1979), 151.

15. Tocqueville stated: "Individualism is a mature and calm feeling, which disposes each member of the community to sever himself from the mass of his fellows and to draw apart with his family and his friends." Although, as always, Tocqueville seemed ambivalent about the moral efficacy of this peculiarly American trait, he leaned toward disapproval. Democratic individualists "owe nothing to any man, they expect nothing from any man; they acquire the habit of always considering themselves standing alone, and they are apt to imagine that their whole destiny is in their own hands" (Alexis de Tocqueville, *Democracy in America*, vol. 2, trans. Henry Reeve [New York: Alfred A. Knopf, 1946], 98–99).

16. Ibid., vol. 1, 406.

17. This point is made by Garry Wills in his essay "The Words That Remade America," *Atlantic Monthly* 269 (June 1992): 79.

18. See, for example, Merle Curti et al., *An American History*, vol. 1 (New York: Harper and Brothers, 1950), 538, 596.

19. In *Keywords*, 213, Raymond Williams points to the eighteenth-century emergence of "nation," where it begins to mean a people grouped under the auspices of political organization rather than older notions of race.

20. In *Nationalism: Problems concerning the Word, the Concept and Classification* (Jyväskylä: Kustantajat, 1964), 48, Aira Kemiläinen reports that nationalism "does not seem to have been very frequently used before the end of the 19th Century."

21. Wallace Evan Davies, *Patriotism on Parade: The Story of Veterans' and Hereditary Organizations in America, 1783-1900* (Cambridge: Harvard University Press, 1955), 216.

22. Cawelti, *Apostles of the Self-Made Man*, 103–6.

23. *Black-Belt Diamonds: Gems from the Speeches, Addresses, and Talks to Students of Booker T. Washington*, ed. Victoria Earle Matthews (New York: Fortune and Scott, 1898), 60.

24. Mary Antin, *They Who Knock at Our Gates: A Complete Gospel of Immigration* (Boston: Houghton Mifflin, 1914), 76.

25. In fact, as Irvin Wyllie discovered, 80 percent of all success manuals published during the nineteenth century appeared after the Civil War (see Wyllie, *The Self-Made Man in America*, 117). The point I want to make here is that national culture is dependent on the spread of print-capitalism, as Benedict Anderson argues in *Imagined Communities: Reflections on the Origin and Spread of Nationalism* (London: Verso, 1983), 30, because it provides "the technical means for 're-presenting' the *kind* of imagined community that is the nation."

26. Tom Nairn, *The Break-Up of Britain*, rev. ed. (London: Verso, 1981), 340.

27. Horatio Alger Jr., *Ragged Dick; or, Street Life in New York* (Boston: A. K. Loring, 1868), 13–14.

28. Alan Trachtenberg writes: "Railroad companies were the earliest giant corporations, the field of enterprise in which first appeared a new breed of men—the Cookes, Stanfords, Huntingtons, and Hills—of unprecedented personal wealth and untrammeled power" (Alan Trachtenberg, *The Incorporation of America: Culture and Society in the Gilded Age* [New York: Hill and Wang, 1982], 57).

29. Alger, *Ragged Dick*, 294. Earlier in the story, the reader is informed that Mickey Maguire has a prior criminal record, having been in prison "two or three times for stealing" (197).

30. Edna Ferber, *Emma McChesney & Co.* (New York: Frederick A. Stokes, 1915), 39.

31. Nevin O. Winter, *Argentina and Her People of To-day* (Boston: Page, 1911), viii, 362, 365–66. Winter's concerns were trumpeted in self-improvement magazines; see, for example, Charles Lyon Chandler, "The World Race for the Rich South American Trade," *World's Work* 25 (January 1913): 314–22.

32. Ferber, *Emma McChesney & Co.*, 8, 9, 13, 14, 31, 39, 43.

33. Warren I. Susman, "'Personality' and the Making of Twentieth-Century Culture," in *Culture as History: The Transformation of American Society in the Twentieth Century* (New York: Pantheon, 1984), 271–85.

34. See A. Whitney Griswold, "Three Puritans on Prosperity," *New England Quarterly* 7 (1934): 475–93.

35. Franklin, *Autobiography*, 73.

36. Robert C. Cushman, quoted in Wyllie, *The Self-Made Man in America*, 21.

37. Ibid., 60.

38. Henry Ward Beecher, quoted in ibid., 156.

39. Ralph Waldo Emerson, quoted in Susman, "'Personality' and the Making of Twentieth-Century Culture," 274.

40. Theodore Roosevelt, "Character and Success," *Outlook* 64 (31 March 1900): 725–27.

41. Take, for example, statements made by two of Roosevelt's contemporaries. Andrew Carnegie, commenting on the "new race" of Americans, claimed: "It may, however, safely be averred that the small mixture of foreign races is a decided advantage to the new [American] race, for even the British race is improved by a slight cross" (Andrew Carnegie, *Triumphant Democracy; or, Fifty Years' March of the Republic* [New York: Charles Scribner's Sons, 1886], 26). Historian Frederick Jackson Turner conflated race and nation in his influential "Frontier Thesis," where he asserted that the "immigrants [are] Americanized, liberated, and fused into a mixed race," with

the result being a "composite nationality for the American people" (Frederick Jackson Turner, "The Significance of the Frontier in American History," in *The Early Writings of Frederick Jackson Turner* [Madison: University of Wisconsin Press, 1938], 211).

42. Andrew Carnegie, *The Empire of Business* (New York: Doubleday, Page, 1902), 129.

43. Booker T. Washington, *Up From Slavery*, in *Three Negro Classics* (New York: Avon, 1965), 46.

44. Raymond Williams, *Marxism and Literature* (New York: Oxford University Press, 1977), 122.

45. It should be noted, however, that outward appearance was an aspect of self-making in its earliest manifestations. Benjamin Franklin, for example, in the midst of invoking the concept of character for entrepreneurial success, advises his students to pay attention to outer image: "In order to secure my Credit and Character as a Tradesman, I took care not only to be in *Reality* Industrious and frugal, but to avoid all *Appearances* of the Contrary. I dressed plainly" (Franklin, *Autobiography*, 54). Although the self-promoting "I" of P. T. Barnum's first autobiography, *The Life of P. T. Barnum, Written by Himself* (1855), proves to be something of an exception to the reign of "character" in nineteenth-century narratives of individual success, the more tempered "self" in *Struggles and Triumphs, or Forty Years' Recollections of P. T. Barnum, Written by Himself* (1869) more readily conforms to this rule.

46. Weiss, *The American Myth of Success*, 133; Cawelti, *Apostles of the Self-Made Man*, 183.

47. Bruce Barton, *The Man Nobody Knows: A Discovery of the Real Jesus* (Indianapolis: Bobbs-Merrill, 1925), 19.

48. Edna Ferber, *Personality Plus: Some Experiences of Emma McChesney and Her Son, Jock* (New York: Frederick A. Stokes, 1914), 51–52.

49. Ferber, *Emma McChesney & Co.*, 42.

50. Younghill Kang, *East Goes West: The Making of an Oriental Yankee* (New York: Charles Scribner's Sons, 1937), 154, 156.

51. Elizabeth Wilson, *Adorned in Dreams: Fashion and Modernity* (Berkeley: University of California Press, 1987), 12.

52. Ferber, *Emma McChesney & Co.*, 38.

53. See Pitirim Sorokin, "American Millionaires and Multi-Millionaires: A Comparative Statistical Study," *Journal of Social Forces* 3 (May 1925): 627–40; William Miller, "American Historians and the Business Elite," *Journal of Economic History* 9 (November 1949): 184–208; Frances W. Gregory and Irene D. Neu, "The American Industrial Elite in the 1870s," *Men in Business: Essays in the History of Entrepreneurship*, ed. William Miller (Cambridge: Harvard University Press, 1952), 193–211.

54. See, for example, Felicity A. Nussbaum, *The Autobiographical Subject: Gender and Ideology in Eighteenth-Century England* (Baltimore: Johns Hopkins University Press, 1989).

55. My study makes no attempt to reconstruct the entire life of each individual under consideration. Instead, the book focuses on each (real or imagined) individual's use of the narrative of self-made success to depict the experience of class mobility. Some chapters also consider instances where the individual explicitly advocates a scheme for entrepreneurial uplift directed at his or her aspiring audience.

1. Class Mobility

1. My discussion of Alger's Progressive Era readership is drawn from Gary Scharnhorst with Jack Bales's informative Afterword to *The Lost Life of Horatio Alger, Jr.* (Bloomington: Indiana University Press, 1985), 149–56.

2. Richard Weiss, *The American Myth of Success: From Horatio Alger to Norman Vincent Peale* (New York: Basic Books, 1969), 49.

3. Horatio Alger Jr., *Ragged Dick; or, Street Life in New York* (Boston: A. K. Loring, 1868), 293.

4. John G. Cawelti, *Apostles of the Self-Made Man* (Chicago: University of Chicago Press, 1965), 110.

5. Robert H. Wiebe, *The Search for Order, 1877–1920* (New York: Hill and Wang, 1967); see also Alan Trachtenberg, *The Incorporation of America: Culture and Society in the Gilded Age* (New York: Hill and Wang, 1982).

6. Andrew Carnegie, "Wealth and Its Uses," in *The Empire of Business* (New York: Doubleday, Page, 1902), 125–26. See also Carnegie's "The Advantages of Poverty," in *The Gospel of Wealth and Other Timely Essays* (Garden City, N.Y.: Doubleday, Doran, 1933), 43–76.

7. Bernard Williams, *Moral Luck: Philosophical Papers, 1973–1980* (Cambridge: Cambridge University Press, 1981), 20–39.

8. Andrew Carnegie, "Introduction: How I Served My Apprenticeship," in *The Gospel of Wealth*, ix.

9. Andrew Carnegie, *Autobiography of Andrew Carnegie* (Boston: Houghton Mifflin, 1920), 34–35. All further references to this work will be included in the text.

10. Andrew Carnegie to the U.S. Military and Old Time Telegraph Association, 10 August 1896. Quoted in Joseph Frazier Wall, *Andrew Carnegie* (New York: Oxford University Press, 1970), 90.

11. Carnegie, "Introduction: How I Served My Apprenticeship," in *The Gospel of Wealth*, xii.

12. Alger, *Ragged Dick*, 65.

13. Ibid., 197. It is difficult to overlook the fact that Mickey's name is almost synonymous with the infamous Molly Maguires, an alleged terrorist organization connected to organized Irish miners in Pennsylvania, who reached public notoriety less than a decade after the appearance of *Ragged Dick* but who were already rumored to exist around the time of the book's initial publication.

14. Quoted in Cawelti, *Apostles of the Self-Made Man*, 111.

15. Ibid., 110.

16. Workers and capitalists, particularly during the 1870s and 1880s, battled over the meaning of democracy and industrialism, as well as the distribution of private property and profits. Many workers responded to the demise of craft production and the ascension of the factory system by adhering to a republican ideology that emphasized community over new forms of individualism, fought for the equal rights of all citizens (usually extending only as far as white men), and battled against the corrupting influence of large inequalities in wealth. Corporate capitalists had an alternative vision of American society. Men such as Carnegie, for example, wanted to place profit and the accumulation of vast fortunes in the moral service of middle-

class notions of progress. For a discussion of labor republicanism within the context of Carnegie's business empire, see Paul Krause, *The Battle for Homestead, 1880–1892: Politics, Culture, and Steel* (Pittsburgh: University of Pittsburgh Press, 1992).

17. One reason Homestead has such a prominent place in U.S. labor history is that it took place within the Carnegie empire. Unlike other robber barons of his era, Carnegie relentlessly portrayed himself as a friend of the workingman despite his conflicting financial interests. On many occasions, he insisted on preserving the dignity of the poor and laboring classes; he went so far as to publicly support the right for workingmen to unionize. Yet, although he claimed to disagree with Frick's violent tactics, Carnegie insisted on the same end—the dissolution of the union at Homestead.

18. Biographer Joseph Frazier Wall suggests that Carnegie, suffering from either poor or selective memory, misrepresents in the *Autobiography* his movements abroad during the Homestead strike as well as his knowledge of the strike during this period (see Wall, *Andrew Carnegie*, 575). My discussion of Carnegie's involvement in the Homestead strike is partly drawn from Wall's treatment of the same in his chapter entitled "Homestead 1892."

19. Ibid., 576.

20. This description of McLuckie is provided in Burton J. Hendrick, *The Life of Andrew Carnegie* (London: William Heinemann, 1933), 340.

21. Daniel T. Rodgers, *The Work Ethic in Industrial America, 1850–1920* (Chicago: University of Chicago Press, 1978), 39.

22. Michael Denning, *Mechanic Accents: Dime Novels and Working-Class Culture in America* (New York: Verso, 1987), 173, 136.

23. James J. Davis, *The Iron Puddler: My Life in the Rolling Mills and What Came of It* (Indianapolis: Bobbs-Merrill, 1922), 17. All further references to this work will be included in the text.

24. Denning, *Mechanic Accents*, 175.

25. Davis develops his nativist position in the essay "Our Labor Shortage and Immigration," *Industrial Management* 65 (June 1923): 321–23.

2. Gender Stability

1. Michael Moon, "'The Gentle Boy from the Dangerous Classes': Pederasty, Domesticity, and Capitalism in Horatio Alger," *Representations* 19 (summer 1987): 87–110.

2. Horatio Alger Jr., *Tattered Tom; or, The Story of a Street Arab* (Boston: A. K. Loring, 1871), 9–10. All further references to this work will be included in the text.

3. For a discussion of Alger's relationship to Charles Loring Brace's Children's Aid Society, see Gary Scharnhorst with Jack Bales, *The Lost Life of Horatio Alger, Jr.* (Bloomington: Indiana University Press, 1985), 78, 80, 111. For an analysis of the effects of such reform institutions on girls, see Christine Stansell, *City of Women: Sex and Class in New York, 1789–1860* (Urbana: University of Illinois Press, 1987).

4. Irvin G. Wyllie, *The Self-Made Man in America: The Myth of Rags to Riches* (New Brunswick, N.J.: Rutgers University Press, 1954), 30–31.

5. Some combination of these scenarios was the case for medicine manufac-

turer Lydia Pinkham, rancher Henrietta King, newspaper mogul Eliza Nicholson, and secretarial school founder Katherine Gibbs. For sketches of the lives of these women, see Caroline Bird, *Enterprising Women* (New York: Norton, 1976).

6. The most complete account of Harriet Hubbard Ayer's life and career is contained in Margaret Hubbard Ayer and Isabella Taves, *The Three Lives of Harriet Hubbard Ayer* (New York: J. B. Lippincott, 1957). Biographical overviews of Ayer can be found in Bernard A. Weisberger's entry in *Notable American Women, 1607–1950*, ed. Edward T. James et al. (Cambridge: Harvard University Press, 1971), 72–74, as well as in Bird, *Enterprising Women*, 127–30.

7. Quoted in Ayer and Taves, *The Three Lives of Harriet Hubbard Ayer*, 119–20.

8. *New York Times*, 28 February 1893, 1.

9. Quoted in Ayer and Taves, *The Three Lives of Harriet Hubbard Ayer*, 160.

10. Quoted in ibid., 162.

11. *New York Herald*, 21 May 1889, 3.

12. Ibid.

13. See *New York Times*, 28 May 1889, 8; *New York Herald*, 28 May 1889, 5.

14. *New York Times*, 28 February 1893, 1.

15. Ayer and Taves assert that the courts granted a child custody injunction based, in part, on Herbert Ayer's plea that "his wife entertained men at her home in the evening for business conferences" (*The Three Lives of Harriet Hubbard Ayer*, 213).

16. In Caroline Bird's brief sketch of turn-of-the-century money-market speculator Hetty Green, she describes the impossibility of the cult of true womanhood squaring with a woman's entrepreneurial ambition: "Hetty has come down in history as a psychopath, but equally paranoid male speculators have been called merely eccentric." Bird rightly concludes: "Whatever the facts behind these images, they reflect the nineteenth-century stereotype that accepted lapses from morality, and even sanity, in men who made money" but not in women (*Enterprising Women*, 87).

17. Edna Ferber, *Roast Beef, Medium: The Business Adventures of Emma McChesney* (New York: Frederick A. Stokes, 1913), 198–99. All further references to this work, abbreviated *RB*, will be included in the text.

18. Edna Ferber, *Personality Plus: Some Experiences of Emma McChesney and Her Son, Jock* (New York: Frederick A. Stokes, 1914), 58. All further references to this work, abbreviated *PP*, will be included in the text.

19. Nancy Armstrong, *Desire and Domestic Fiction: A Political History of the Novel* (New York: Oxford University Press, 1987).

20. Note that the U.S. census indicates that, during the 1910s, the number of women employed as traveling sales agents actually declined relative to the prior decade. See "Table 115: Women Employed in Each Specified Occupation . . . 1920," in Joseph A. Hill, *Women in Gainful Occupations, 1870–1920* (Washington, D.C.: U.S. Government Printing Office, 1929), 180–81. In fact, women were two and one-half times less likely to be sales agents in 1920 than in 1910. Alternatively, the number of saleswomen inside stores (whose numbers, in 1920, were more than two hundred times greater than those of traveling sales agents) showed a marked increase over their numbers in 1910.

21. Edna Ferber, *Emma McChesney & Co.* (New York: Frederick A. Stokes,

1915), 178. All further references to this work, abbreviated *EM*, will be included in the text.

22. Helen Christene Hoerle and Florence B. Saltzberg, *The Girl and the Job* (New York: Henry Holt, 1919), 5.

23. In a chapter titled "The Girl in Industry," Hoerle and Saltzberg suggest that "more women are employed in the clothing industries than in all the others combined" (a trend that would continue until 1940). The authors do state, however, that women remain largely excluded from the field of commercial travel. "Until very recently," they acknowledge, a woman's "capability for selling merchandise" on the road "was doubted." Furthermore, conventional wisdom suggested "that the incessant traveling necessary in this kind of work was too wearing for a woman" (Hoerle and Saltzberg, *The Girl and the Job*, 103, 224).

24. Ibid., 105. In appropriating Ferber's literary character Emma McChesney as their model for the successful saleswoman, Hoerle and Saltzberg bypass the forty-three female professional consultants (whose fields of employment range from stenographer to statistician but none of whom is a commercial traveler) listed in the book's acknowledgments.

25. "Emma McChesney," review of *Emma McChesney & Co.*, *New York Times Book Review* (17 October 1915): 390.

26. Hoerle and Saltzberg, *The Girl and the Job*, 105.

27. "Personality Plus," review of *Personality Plus*, *New York Times Book Review* (20 September 1914): 386.

28. Ferber's uneasiness with contemporary feminism is evident in a *New York Times* interview that appeared in the same year as *Emma McChesney & Co.* See Julie Goldsmith Gilbert, *Ferber: A Biography* (Garden City, N.Y.: Doubleday, 1978), 409. In *Emma McChesney & Co.*, the title character is heard scolding affluent and apparently out-of-touch feminist reformers who lobby on behalf of uplifting the working girl.

29. "Vaudeville Sketches of the Business Woman," review of *Roast Beef, Medium*, *Current Opinion* 54 (June 1913): 491.

30. *American Magazine* 75 (December 1912): 107. In fact, Roosevelt did not write this letter to Ferber. However, in a letter to Ferber dated 4 December 1912, Roosevelt happily confirmed that he said these things: "I did make those statements and I am rather proud that it should be publicly known that I had such good taste!" See *The Letters of Theodore Roosevelt*, vol. 7, ed. Elting E. Morison (Cambridge: Harvard University Press, 1954), 661.

31. *American Magazine* 75 (April 1913): 5.

32. "Emma McChesney," *New York Times Book Review*, 390.

3. Racial Segregation

1. W. E. B. Du Bois, "Results of the Investigation," *The Negro in Business: A Social Study Made under the Direction of the Atlanta University by the Fourth Atlanta Conference*, ed. W. E. B. Du Bois (Atlanta: Press of Atlanta University, 1899), 5.

2. Ibid., 6.

3. Ibid., 15.

4. "Resolutions Adopted by the Conference," in *The Negro in Business*, 50.

5. Ida B. Wells, *Crusade for Justice: The Autobiography of Ida B. Wells*, ed. Alfreda M. Duster (Chicago: University of Chicago Press, 1970), 64.

6. Ibid., 21. William T. Adams, author of Oliver Optic's boy's stories, was the editor of *Student and Schoolmate*. He worked alongside his close friend Horatio Alger Jr. in helping the latter conceive the "luck and pluck" formula, and then proceeded to use it himself. Under the nom de plume Oliver Optic, Adams published a number of boy's stories with Alger-inspired formulas, such as *Desk and Debit; or, The Catastrophes of a Clerk* (1873). It is no coincidence that Alger's *Ragged Dick*, which propelled the author to fame and fortune, was initially serialized in January 1867 issues of *Student and Schoolmate*. For a discussion of the personal and professional relationship between Adams and Alger, see Edwin P. Hoyt, *Horatio's Boys: The Life and Works of Horatio Alger, Jr.* (Radnor, Pa.: Chilton Book Co., 1974), 73–74.

7. Wells, *Crusade for Justice*, 32.

8. Ibid., 47.

9. Ida B. Wells, *A Red Record: Tabulated Statistics and Alleged Causes of Lynchings in the United States, 1892–1893–1894* (1895), in *Selected Works of Ida B. Wells-Barnett* (New York: Oxford, 1991), 219.

10. Wells, *Crusade for Justice*, 48.

11. In *Southern Horrors*—Ida B. Wells's first attempt outside a newspaper format to make public the racist logic behind lynching—she quotes angry whites in Memphis as saying: "The Negroes are getting too independent . . . we must teach them a lesson" (*Southern Horrors: Lynch Law in All Its Phases* [1892], in *Selected Works of Ida B. Wells-Barnett*, 36).

12. Ibid., 40.

13. Ibid., 45.

14. Wells reported that, prior to the turn of the century, lynchings peaked in the year 1892 at 241. See Ida B. Wells, *Mob Rule in New Orleans: Robert Charles and His Fight to the Death* (1900), in ibid., 320.

15. Booker T. Washington, *Up From Slavery*, in *Three Negro Classics* (New York: Avon, 1965), 71. All further references to *Up From Slavery* will be included in the text.

16. For an overview of the reception of *Up From Slavery*, see Louis R. Harlan, *Booker T. Washington: The Making of a Black Leader, 1856–1901* (New York: Oxford University Press, 1972), 249–53.

17. Recall that Washington's close ally, Andrew Carnegie (whom Washington trusted as "one of the dearest and best friends I ever had" [Booker T. Washington to Andrew Carnegie, 7 December 1906; quoted in Louis R. Harlan, *Booker T. Washington: The Wizard of Tuskegee, 1901–1915* (New York: Oxford University Press, 1983), 138]), was very fond of preaching that "poverty" rather than affluence was nothing less than a righteous "school" for preparing the disadvantaged for success. See, for instance, Carnegie's 1891 article titled "The Advantages of Poverty," in *The Gospel of Wealth and Other Timely Essays* (Garden City, N.Y.: Doubleday, Doran, 1933).

18. See Roy P. Basler, *The Lincoln Legend: A Study in Changing Conceptions* (Boston: Houghton Mifflin, 1935).

19. Booker T. Washington, *My Larger Education: Being Chapters from My Experience* (Garden City, N.Y.: Doubleday, Page, 1911), 106.

20. As historian August Meier cautions, Washington's rise to national prominence was the result not of the originality of his proposals, "but because his program had already become the core of the thought of influential groups in the North, in the South, and among Negroes" (Meier, *Negro Thought in America, 1880–1915: Racial Ideologies in the Age of Booker T. Washington* [Ann Arbor: University of Michigan Press, 1969], 99).

21. Booker T. Washington, *The Negro in Business* (Boston: Hertel, Jenkins, 1907), 4. See also Washington's collection of speeches titled *Black-Belt Diamonds*, ed. Victoria Earle Matthews (New York: Fortune and Scott, 1898).

22. Michel Foucault, *Discipline and Punish: The Birth of the Prison*, trans. Alan Sheridan (New York: Vintage, 1979), 137.

23. Andrew Carnegie stated that no individual represented the rags-to-riches American success story better than Booker T. Washington. In his *Autobiography* (Boston: Houghton Mifflin, 1920), 276–77, Carnegie writes: "We should all take our hats off to the man who not only raised himself from slavery but helped raise millions of his race to a higher stage of civilization." He elaborates on the remarkable career of Washington as follows: "No truer, more self-sacrificing hero ever lived: a man compounded of all the virtues. . . . If it be asked which man of our age, or even of the past ages, has risen from the lowest to the highest, the answer must be Booker Washington. He rose from slavery to the leadership of his people—a modern Moses and Joshua combined, leading his people both onward and upward." Carnegie's leadership role in funding the NNBL is referenced in August Meier's *Negro Thought in America*, 124.

24. *Report of the Thirteenth Annual Convention of the National Negro Business League* (Nashville: Sunday School Union Print, 1912), 154.

25. Ibid.

26. Ibid., 155.

27. Louis Harlan provides a discussion of Washington's limited role in the development of colonial Africa in *Booker T. Washington: The Wizard of Tuskegee, 1901–1915*, 266–94.

28. Despite their awareness of the crimes committed against Africans throughout the world in the name of progress, black leaders—ranging from the Reverend Alexander Crummell to Booker T. Washington—appropriated the European language of the civilizing mission in their attempt to bring Africa into the modern world. For an account of the "civilizationist" tradition within black nationalism, see Wilson Jeremiah Moses, *The Golden Age of Black Nationalism, 1850–1925* (New York: Oxford University Press, 1988).

29. *Report of the Thirteenth Annual Convention of the National Negro Business League*, 154.

30. For an analysis of black women's employment in the South at the turn of the century, see Jacqueline Jones, *Labor of Love, Labor of Sorrow: Black Women, Work, and the Family from Slavery to the Present* (New York: Basic Books, 1985).

31. *Report of the Thirteenth Annual Convention of the National Negro Business League*, 154–55.

32. The *Indianapolis Freeman* provided Walker extensive press coverage from the time she moved her business operations to Indiana in 1910 until her death in 1919. On this day, the newspaper ran three separate stories on Walker: the aforementioned front-page biography, which both opened by erroneously giving the day of her birth as 25 December 1867 and included a flattering photo of Walker over the caption: "The best known Hair Culturist in America"; a page-two photojournalist piece depicting the operations of the Walker Manufacturing Company, Inc.; and, a page-four lifestyles article titled "Mme. C. J. Walker. A Review of a Remarkable Business Woman and Her Brilliant Career."

33. *Indianapolis Freeman*, 11 November 1911, 1.

34. Ibid.

35. Conventional gender assignments at NNBL gatherings are indicated in a 1909 open letter signed by Washington and addressed to black newspapers that advertised the upcoming tenth annual convention. Although Washington "urge[d] the attendance of men and women of our race engaged in business throughout the country," he made a special plea to businessmen: "We hope that the men will not only be present in large numbers but, if possible, they will bring their wives and other members of their families" (*Indianapolis Freeman*, 3 July 1909, 3).

36. *Report of the Eighteenth and Nineteenth Annual Sessions of the National Negro Business League* (Nashville: Baptist Publishing Board, n.d.), 77.

37. Hazel V. Carby, *Reconstructing Womanhood: The Emergence of the Afro-American Woman Novelist* (New York: Oxford University Press, 1987).

38. *Indianapolis Freeman*, 28 December 1912, 16.

39. *Report of the Fourteenth Annual Convention of the National Negro Business League* (Nashville: Sunday School Union Print, 1913), 210.

40. A'Lelia Perry Bundles, *Madam C. J. Walker* (New York: Chelsea House, 1991), 15.

41. *Report of the Fourteenth Annual Convention of the National Negro Business League*, 210.

42. Ibid., 211.

43. During the same year, for example, one woman wrote her: "You have opened up a trade for hundreds of colored women to make an honest and profitable living where they make as much in one week as a month's salary would bring from any other position that a colored woman can secure" (quoted in A'Lelia Perry Bundles, "Madam C. J. Walker—Cosmetics Tycoon," *Ms.* 11 [July 1983], 93).

44. *Report of the Fourteenth Annual Convention of the National Negro Business League*, 212.

45. *Indianapolis Freeman*, 26 December 1914, 1.

46. *Report of the Fifteenth Annual Convention of the National Negro Business League* (Nashville: Sunday School Union Print, 1914), 153.

47. *Report of the Seventeenth Annual Convention of the National Negro Business League* (Nashville: National Baptist Publishing Board, 1916), 134.

48. *Indianapolis Freeman*, 16 April 1910, 2.

49. Walker, quoted in Bundles, "Madam C. J. Walker—Cosmetics Tycoon," 92.

50. *Report of the Fifteenth Annual Convention of the National Negro Business League*, 152.

51. ILDP, quoted in Judith Stein, *The World of Marcus Garvey: Race and Class in Modern Society* (Baton Rouge: Louisiana State University Press, 1986), 50.

52. *Denver Post*, 11 July 1918, 13.

53. Prior to desegregation, Madam Walker was repeatedly celebrated in black newspapers and magazines for her accomplishments as a Negro and a woman, a millionaire and a philanthropist. The readers of *Ebony*, for instance, in celebration of Black History Week during February 1956, chose Madam Walker as their first inductee into the monthly magazine's Hall of Fame. See *Ebony* 11 (February 1956): 25.

54. A'Lelia Bundles, quoted from personal correspondence. In addition, Bundles states that, given Walker's vocal support for the NAACP's antilynching campaign in the mid-teens, "one would think that she would have capitalized on such a life-defining event to help the cause."

4. Immigrant Aspirations

1. "Will Stand by Slogan 'Africa for the Africans at Home and Abroad,'" *Negro World*, 17 September 1921, in *The Marcus Garvey and Universal Negro Improvement Association Papers*, ed. Robert A. Hill, 10 vols. projected (Berkeley: University of California Press, 1983–), vol. 4, 35.

2. "Convention Report," *Negro World*, 2 September 1922, in ibid., 940.

3. *Black-Belt Diamonds: Gems from the Speeches, Addresses, and Talks to Students of Booker T. Washington*, ed. Victoria Earle Matthews (New York: Fortune and Scott, 1898), 60.

4. Marcus Garvey, *Philosophy and Opinions of Marcus Garvey*, ed. Amy Jacques Garvey, 2 vols. (1926; rpt. Totawa, N.J.: Frank Cass, 1967), vol. 2, 23. Garvey reproduced this quote in a full front-page statement carried in the 29 January 1927 *Negro World*. It appeared this time under the equally blunt title "Momentum of Progress Will Batter Down the Prejudice against Negroes—Nothing Succeeds like Success."

5. Garvey, quoted in Rollin Lynde Hartt, "The Negro Moses and His Campaign to Lead the Black Millions into Their Promised Land," *Independent* 105 (26 February 1921): 206.

6. Garvey's biographers are in general agreement about the lack of reliable information, autobiographical or otherwise, in regard to his boyhood. Under the heading "Autobiography," Robert A. Hill has collected Garvey's postdeportation recollections of his years in the United States as head of the UNIA, which were printed in the February through May 1930 editions of the *Pittsburgh Courier*. See *Marcus Garvey: Life and Lessons: A Centennial Companion to the Marcus Garvey and Universal Negro Improvement Association Papers*, ed. Robert A. Hill (Berkeley: University of California Press, 1987), 33–114. In the tradition of Ben Franklin's memoirs, Garvey stated: "I am giving this rehearsal of what ha[s] happened to the Black Star Line with the hope of helping other business men" (69).

7. Robert A. Hill, "General Introduction," in *The Marcus Garvey and Universal Negro Improvement Association Papers*, vol. 1, lxxxiii.

8. Marcus Garvey, "The Negro's Greatest Enemy," *Current History* 18 (September 1923): 951.

9. Ibid., 952.

10. Ibid.

11. Booker T. Washington to Marcus Garvey, 27 April 1915. The letter is reproduced in *The Marcus Garvey and Universal Negro Improvement Association Papers*, vol. 1, 118.

12. Louis R. Harlan, *Booker T. Washington: The Wizard of Tuskegee, 1901–1915* (New York: Oxford University Press, 1983), 281.

13. On 3 August 1915, the *Jamaican Daily Chronicle* reported: "The Universal Negro Improvement Association is about taking up and putting through a scheme to establish in Jamaica a large industrial farm and institution on the same plan as the Tuskegee Normal and Industrial Institute of which Dr. Booker T. Washington is head" (*The Marcus Garvey and Universal Negro Improvement Association Papers*, vol. 1, 128).

14. Roscoe Simmons, *Chicago Defender*, 6 September 1924; quoted in Edmund David Cronon, *Black Moses: The Story of Marcus Garvey and the Universal Negro Improvement Association* (Madison: University of Wisconsin Press, 1955), 122.

15. *New York News*, 7 February 1925; quoted in Cronon, *Black Moses*, 136.

16. Garvey, quoted in Du Bois's January 1921 *Crisis* editorial titled "Marcus Garvey"; see W. E. B. Du Bois, *Writings*, ed. Nathan Huggins (New York: Library of America), 976 n. 1.

17. Cronon, *Black Moses*, 51.

18. It is next to impossible to estimate the number of followers of Marcus Garvey during his residency in the United States. While Garvey repeatedly boasted that membership in the Universal Negro Improvement Association was in the millions, Du Bois suggested that the UNIA had approximately eighty thousand members in 1920 (see W. E. B. Du Bois, "Back to Africa," *Century* 105 [February 1923]: 543). Regardless, as Edmund David Cronon points out, "the actual dues-paying membership of the [UNIA] was far smaller than the number of Negroes who identified themselves with the exciting emotional atmosphere of the movement and gave its aim vigorous if informal support" (Cronon, *Black Moses*, 204). Garvey's popularity in the United States peaked sometime between the First UNIA International Convention, held in 1920, and his arrest on mail fraud charges in 1922.

19. *Negro World*, 1 November 1919, in *The Marcus Garvey and Universal Negro Improvement Association Papers*, vol. 2, 94.

20. Garvey, quoted in Hartt, "The Negro Moses and His Campaign to Lead the Black Millions into Their Promised Land," 218.

21. *Negro World*, 8 April 1922, in *The Marcus Garvey and Universal Negro Improvement Association Papers*, vol. 4, 594.

22. In Garvey's postdeportation writings, he states that enterprising women like Madam Walker "have employed thousands of Negroes and found bread for them, thereby helping to lif[t] the economic standard of the race" (*Marcus Garvey: Life and Lessons*, 100).

23. *Negro World*, 17 July 1920, in *The Marcus Garvey and Universal Negro Improvement Association Papers*, vol. 2, 416.

24. Marcus Garvey, "A Talk with Afro-West Indians," circa July–August 1914, in ibid., vol. 1, 55.

25. Garvey, *Philosophy and Opinions of Marcus Garvey*, vol. 2, 23.

26. *Daily Chronicle*, 26 August 1915, in ibid., vol. 1, 132–36.

27. *Daily Chronicle*, 8 September 1915, in ibid., 138.

28. Judith Stein, *The World of Marcus Garvey: Race and Class in Modern Society* (Baton Rouge: Louisiana State University Press, 1986), 11.

29. Ibid., 64–66.

30. Cronon, *Black Moses*, 52.

31. *Negro World*, 1 February 1919, in *The Marcus Garvey and Universal Negro Improvement Association Papers*, vol. 1, 352. In 1930, a few years after leaving the United States, Garvey wistfully reflected on the lost opportunity for black American entrepreneurial imperialism in Africa and elsewhere: "our trade relationship would have been established between our races in Africa, in the United States, in South and Central America and the West Indies; we would have been removing raw materials from plantations of far-off Africa, from South and Central America, and the West Indies, to our factories in the United States, thus giving employment to millions of Negroes in America . . . to millions more in tropical Africa and South and Central America, and the West Indies" (*Marcus Garvey: Life and Lessons*, 91).

32. Quoted from Garvey's speech before the Mount Carmel Baptist Church (Washington, D.C.), 24 July 1920, in *The Marcus Garvey and Universal Negro Improvement Association Papers*, vol. 2, 458. For an analysis of Garveyism within a transnational framework, see Paul Gilroy, *The Black Atlantic: Modernity and Double Consciousness* (Cambridge: Harvard University Press, 1993).

33. *Negro World*, 9 September 1922, in *The Marcus Garvey and Universal Negro Improvement Association Papers*, vol. 4, 1055.

34. Hill, "General Introduction," in ibid., vol. 1, 1.

35. Garvey, *Philosophy and Opinions of Marcus Garvey*, vol. 2, 65.

36. Ibid., vol. 1, 68.

37. Ibid., 67.

38. See Marcus Garvey, "Hail! United States of Africa!" in *The Tragedy of White Injustice*, ed. Amy Jacques Garvey (New York: Amy Jacques Garvey, 1927), 20–21.

39. *Negro World*, 17 July 1920, in *The Marcus Garvey and Universal Negro Improvement Association Papers*, vol. 2, 414.

40. In the 1880s, the peak decade of nineteenth-century immigration, 72 percent of the immigrants still originated from northern and western Europe. By the first decade of the twentieth century, the peak decade in the history of American immigration, 72 percent were from southern and eastern Europe. See U.S., Congress, Senate, *Abstracts of Reports of the Immigration Commission, with Conclusions and Recommendations and Views of the Minority*, S Doc. 747, 61 Cong. 3d sess., 1911, 1:57, 64.

41. John Higham, *Strangers in the Land: Patterns of American Nativism, 1860–1925*, 2d ed. (New York: Atheneum, 1975), 33.

42. Andrew Carnegie, *Triumphant Democracy; or, Fifty Years' March of the Republic* (New York: Charles Scribner's Sons, 1886), 23. Carnegie calculated that four out of five Americans had British ancestry, while the other fifth was principally German. Although he professed in the mid-1880s that immigration from other countries was "scarcely worth taking into account," he assured his audience of the benign and even beneficial influence of "foreign races" on the national character: "It may,

however, safely be averred that the small mixture of foreign races is a decided advantage to the new [American] race, for even the British race is improved by a slight cross." The American people, Carnegie optimistically concluded, "are ever becoming more purely British in origin" (25–26, 34).

43. Higham, *Strangers in the Land*, chapter 6.

44. U.S., Congress, Senate, *Abstracts of Reports of the Immigration Commission*, 1:12–14.

45. Mary Antin, *They Who Knock at Our Gates: A Complete Gospel of Immigration* (Boston: Houghton Mifflin, 1914), 98, 9–10.

46. Nevertheless, Antin probably could not help but notice that, during the Gilded Age, although Wall Street financier J. P. Morgan might be a household name, Bank of America founder A. P. Giannini (son of northern Italian immigrants) climbed the ladder of success in relative obscurity.

47. Antin, *They Who Knock at Our Gates*, 76.

48. Mary Antin, *The Promised Land* (Boston: Houghton Mifflin, 1912), xix. All further references to this work will be included in the text.

49. Oscar Handlin reports that, at the time of the publication of *The Promised Land*, Antin was "a young and virtually unknown author." After being serialized in the *Atlantic Monthly*, the book "met an enthusiastic reception and sold some 85,000 copies in 34 printings." See Handlin's 1969 Foreword to *The Promised Land* (Princeton, N.J.: Princeton University Press, 1985), v.

50. Allen Guttmann, for example, in his seminal analysis of Jewish writers in the United States, concludes that Antin's "gratitude for her own success had, of course, led her to considerable underestimation of the difficulties faced by less gifted immigrants" (Guttmann, *The Jewish Writer in America: Assimilation and the Crisis of Identity* [New York: Oxford University Press, 1971], 28).

51. Late in *The Promised Land* we learn that, unlike Mary, Dora gladly joins a club designed to instruct girls in domestic science: "The leader of this club, under pretense of teaching the little girls the proper way to sweep and make beds, artfully teaches them how to beautify a tenement home by means of noble living" (325).

52. Emerson describes the higher laws of the Oversoul in the following way: "that great nature in which we rest . . . that Unity, that Over-soul, within which every man's particular being is contained and made one with all other" (Ralph Waldo Emerson, "The Over-Soul," in *The Complete Works of Ralph Waldo Emerson* [Boston: Houghton Mifflin, 1904], vol. 2, 268).

53. Emerson invokes the "self-helping man" in his essay "Self-Reliance," in ibid., 78. For an extended treatment of Emerson as a philosopher of self-reliance and success, see John G. Cawelti, *Apostles of the Self-Made Man* (Chicago: University of Chicago Press, 1965), 86–98.

54. The fact that Kang's novels *East Goes West* and *The Grass Roof* are thinly veiled autobiographies is confirmed in an autobiographical essay titled "Oriental Yankee," *Common Ground* 1 (winter 1941): 59–63.

55. Younghill Kang, *East Goes West: The Making of an Oriental Yankee* (New York: Charles Scribner's Sons, 1937), 5. All further references to this work will be included in the text.

56. Younghill Kang, *The Grass Roof* (New York: Charles Scribner's Sons, 1931), 339.

57. Oscar Handlin, *The Uprooted*, 2d ed. (Boston: Little, Brown, 1979), 223.

58. Elaine H. Kim, "Searching for a Door to America: Younghill Kang, Korean American Writer," *Korea Journal* 17 (April 1977): 39.

59. Kang, *The Grass Roof*, 149.

60. Ibid., 362.

61. See Bruce Barton, *The Man Nobody Knows: A Discovery of the Real Jesus* (Indianapolis: Bobbs-Merrill, 1925).

62. For an extended treatment of the relation between narrative forms and Taylorization within the period under consideration, see Martha Banta's *Taylored Lives: Narrative Productions in the Age of Taylor, Veblen, and Ford* (Chicago: University of Chicago Press, 1993).

63. In *East Goes West*, Kang details the descending hierarchy of department store employment, where women almost always occupy the lowest-paying jobs. The result is a work environment at Boshnack's in which men stereotype women workers as sex objects.

64. Kang, "Oriental Yankee," 61. Toward the end of *East Goes West*, Kang's autobiographical narrator briefly alludes to the fact that noncommercial interests finally displaced his entrepreneurial ambitions. Employed as an expert on Eastern affairs for the *Encyclopedia Britannica* in the late 1920s, Han reflects: "I had aimed. I had dropped. I had captured my little opening . . . in the professional intellectual world" (348). In the autobiographical essay "Oriental Yankee," Kang claimed that (with degrees from Harvard and Boston universities) he devoted his adulthood to "waiting and watching constantly for an opening whereby I, too, might become a part of American intellectual life" (61). However, opportunities in academia never fully opened to him. While a staff member at the Metropolitan Museum of Art in the late 1920s, he taught freshman composition at New York University. At this time his literary talents were "discovered" by Thomas Wolfe, who, after reading his autobiographies, befriended Kang and dubbed him an "Oriental Yankee" (63). Although Kang gained some notoriety and awards during the 1930s for his autobiographical fiction, his inability to secure a tenured position at an American college remained a source of frustration throughout his life. He died in December 1972, at age sixty-nine, in relative obscurity.

65. Sui Sin Far [Edith Maud Eaton], "Tian Shan's Kindred Spirit," in *Mrs. Spring Fragrance* (Chicago: A. C. McClurg, 1912), 234.

66. Although there exists scant recent criticism on *East Goes West*, it is unanimous in its dismissal of the book's conclusion as foolish and lame. See Kim, "Searching for a Door to America," 46; and, James Wade, "Younghill Kang's Unwritten Third Act," in *West Meets East: An Encounter with Korea* (n.p.: Pomso Publishers, 1975), 115.

67. My explication of specific Buddhist principles in this paragraph and the next is indebted to Peter Harvey's *An Introduction to Buddhism: Teachings, History and Practices* (New York: Cambridge University Press, 1990), 44–46, 50–53, 60–61, 65–68.

68. In *The Grass Roof*, Kang offers his fullest account of Nirvana in the form of young Chungpa's instruction by a Buddhist monk: "He tried to teach me the way of Nirvana, which means a 'blowing out,' like a candle." Etched in Han's memory is

a poem inscribed on a monastery's pillar: "Make no evil deed, / All good obediently do. / Purge the mind of self, / This is all Buddha's teaching" (166).

5. Individual Enterprise in the Postfrontier Nation

1. F. Scott Fitzgerald, *The Great Gatsby* (New York: Macmillan, 1992), 6. All further references to this work will be included in the text.

2. Lionel Trilling, *The Liberal Imagination* (Garden City, N.Y.: Doubleday, 1950), 251. William Troy, in his 1945 essay "Scott Fitzgerald—the Authority of Failure" (*Accent* 6 [1945]: 56–60), was the first critic to use the term "American dream" in an interpretation of *The Great Gatsby*.

3. Edwin S. Fussell, "Fitzgerald's Brave New World," *ELH* 19 (1952): 295.

4. Nowhere, institutionally or pedagogically speaking, is the use of these analytical binaries more evident than in the criticism contained under the section headings "Crime and Corruption" and "The American Dream" in the well-worn Scribner Research Anthology titled *Fitzgerald's* Great Gatsby: *The Novel, the Critics, the Background*, ed. Henry Dan Piper (New York: Charles Scribner's Sons, 1970).

5. Marius Bewley, "Scott Fitzgerald's Criticism of America," *Sewanee Review* 62 (1954): 223, 245–46. Bewley's model for interpreting *The Great Gatsby* has found numerous restatements during the subsequent decades.

6. Walter Benn Michaels, "The Vanishing American," *American Literary History* 2 (summer 1990): 224. In the simplest terms, the principal task of Michaels's commentary on classic American literature of the 1920s is to prove his hypothesis that the segregationist question "Are you white?" is "replaced" by the nativist query "Are you American?" Armed with this presupposition, Michaels is unable to adequately account for the irrepressible significance of black/white difference in Jazz Age fiction. See Michaels's "Anti-Imperial Americanism," *Cultures of United States Imperialism*, ed. Amy Kaplan and Donald E. Pease (Durham, N.C.: Duke University Press, 1993), 366; "The Souls of White Folk," *Literature and the Body: Essays on Populations and Persons*, ed. Elaine Scarry (Baltimore: Johns Hopkins University Press, 1988), 192; "The Vanishing American," 235.

7. Fitzgerald confessed the influence of Joseph Conrad on his craft in the Introduction to the 1934 Modern Library Edition of *The Great Gatsby*. Note that Nick echoes no one so much as Conrad's narrator Marlow, and, like *Heart of Darkness*, Fitzgerald's novel neither embraces white supremacy nor ultimately rejects imperialist thought. As Terry Eagleton describes it, Conrad's *Heart of Darkness* conveys the "'message' . . . that Western civilisation is at base as barbarous as African society—a viewpoint which disturbs imperialist assumptions to the precise degree that it reinforces them" (Terry Eagleton, *Criticism and Ideology: A Study of Marxist Literary Theory* [London: Verso, 1978], 135).

8. Eric Lott demonstrates how the minstrel show is structured by "interracial recognitions and identifications no less than the imperative to disavow them" (Eric Lott, *Love and Theft: Blackface Minstrelsy and the American Working Class* [New York: Oxford University Press, 1993], 35).

9. John Higham, *Strangers in the Land: Patterns of American Nativism, 1860–1925*, 2d ed. (New York: Atheneum, 1975), 311.

10. Warren Harding, quoted in W. E. B. Du Bois, "President Harding and Social Equality," in *Writings*, ed. Nathan Huggins (New York: Library of America, 1986), 1194.

11. Ibid.

12. Marcus Garvey, quoted in Robert A. Hill, "General Introduction," in *The Marcus Garvey and Universal Negro Improvement Association Papers*, ed. Robert A. Hill, 10 vols. projected (Berkeley: University of California Press, 1983–), vol. 1, lxxxii.

13. Higham, *Strangers in the Land*, 266–67. This trend was best exemplified in the changing philosophy, membership, and activities of the Ku Klux Klan. The first official postwar Klan appearance did not occur until 1920 and, with the "Red Summer" of 1919 behind it (which witnessed numerous race riots and lynchings), the organization began focusing its attacks on white foreigners. The Klan was not less race-conscious than before but it did introduce a number of changes into its fold. The Knights of the Invisible Empire made extensive use of eugenics to justify its new interest in nativism. Klan activity shifted from exclusive attacks on Negroes to a broad-based hatred of foreigners who seemed less than white, particularly Italians and Jews. For the first time, Klan membership was extended only to native-born Protestant whites. The spread of Klan activities at this moment was reflected in the geographical expansion of its membership from the rural South to the small Midwestern town and the urban North. Moreover, the ranks of Klansmen swelled to unprecedented numbers, estimated at 4.5 million in 1924.

14. Ibid., 265, 273.

15. Kenneth L. Roberts, *Why Europe Leaves Home* (Indianapolis: Bobbs-Merrill, 1922), 22.

16. Calvin Coolidge, quoted in Madison Grant, "America for the Americans," *Forum* 74 (September 1925): 347.

17. C. M. Timpson, "Perverted History," *New York Times*, 30 June 1922, 16.

18. John B. Kennedy, "Who 'Discovered' America," *New York Times*, 4 July 1922, 12.

19. Clinton Stoddard Burr, *America's Race Heritage* (New York: National Historical Society, 1922), 208.

20. *Gatsby* takes place precisely two years after Brolaski ran his illicit alcohol trade from California. On approximately the same date that Fitzgerald has Nick meet Gatsby for the first time (mid- to late June 1922), the *New York Times* published an exposé headlined "Brolaski, Bootleg King—Man Named by Caraway in Senate Attack a Real Millionaire Bootlegger" (Henry J. Rogers, "Brolaski, Bootleg King—Man Named by Caraway in Senate Attack a Real Millionaire Bootlegger" *New York Times*, 18 June 1922 [sec. 7], 6). Perhaps this was additional source material for Fitzgerald's representation of both his narrator and his American hero. Although he does not mention either Harry Brolaski or Senator Caraway, Joseph Corso uncovers other potential sources for Fitzgerald's characters in his "One Not-Forgotten Summer Night: Sources for Fictional Symbols of American Character in *The Great Gatsby*," in *Fitzgerald/Hemingway Annual 1976*, ed. Matthew J. Bruccoli (Englewood, Colo.: Information Handling Services, 1978), 9–33.

21. John M. Kenny Jr., "The Great Gatsby," *Commonweal*, 3 June 1925, 110.

22. Sander L. Gilman, *Difference and Pathology: Stereotypes of Sexuality, Race, and Madness* (Ithaca, N.Y.: Cornell University Press, 1985), 18.

23. In the early 1920s, Nordic philosophers indirectly used the discovery of Indo-European languages as evidence to support their own claims. By tracing America's northwestern European origins to a remote Aryan past, nativist writers of the early twenties distanced the nation's race heritage from what, prior to this discovery, would have been its previous point of departure: Semitic civilization. For instance, Clinton Stoddard Burr opens *America's Race Heritage* with a reference to "the race migrations in Eurasia as a prelude to the racial history of America." In the course of his study, Burr draws the distinction between a superior Aryan Europe family of man and an inferior Hebrew race. See Burr, *America's Race Heritage*, 19.

24. Ibid., 195. It is important to remember that, with a loss of faith in Progressive Era efforts to assimilate immigrants, Jews (as much as if not more than any other new immigrant group) became a national menace in the eyes of postwar nativists. For example, in the early months of 1920, Henry Ford—the country's leading industrialist, folk hero to millions, and onetime melting-pot model advocate—began using his company organ, the *Dearborn Independent*, to wage an anti-Semitic propaganda campaign against what he called "international Financiers" operating in America.

25. Thomas Caldecot Chubb, "Bagdad-on-Subway," *Forum* 74 (August 1925): 311.

26. Gatsby's struggle upward is structured, according to Nick's narrative, along the lines of Horatio Alger Jr.'s popular formula. For a discussion of the relationship between *The Great Gatsby* and Alger's stories, see Gary Scharnhorst, "Scribbling Upward: Fitzgerald's Debt of Honor to Horatio Alger, Jr.," in *Fitzgerald/Hemingway Annual 1978*, eds. Matthew J. Bruccoli and Richard Layman (Detroit: Gale Research, 1979), 161–69.

27. Floyd C. Watkins was the first critic to give extensive treatment to the influence of Franklin's writing on *The Great Gatsby*; see his "Fitzgerald's Jay Gatz and Young Ben Franklin," *New England Quarterly* 17 (1954): 249–52.

28. Richard Weiss, *The American Myth of Success: From Horatio Alger to Norman Vincent Peale* (New York: Basic Books, 1969), 216.

29. Higham, *Strangers in the Land*, 155–56.

30. Grant and his disciples were not alone among nativists in deploying eugenics to construct a national identity base on narrowing definitions of whiteness. The "expert" services of eugenicist Harry H. Laughlin were retained by Congressman Albert Johnson's House Committee on Immigration Restriction, where he testified that new European immigrants were bad breeding stock due to their "inborn socially inadequate qualities." Even presidential hopeful Calvin Coolidge lent his signature to a popular piece on immigration restriction, published in a 1921 issue of *Good Housekeeping*, which used biological laws to argue that Nordic stock degenerates when mixed with other races (ibid., 314, 318).

31. For a discussion of nativist uses of popular images of the New Woman, see Martha Banta, *Imaging American Women: Idea and Ideals in Cultural History* (New York: Columbia University Press, 1987), 104–39.

32. William Rose Benét, "An Admirable Novel," *Saturday Review of Literature* 1 (9 May 1925): 740.

33. Critics have overlooked the possibility that, in addition to Stoddard's book, the well-known geneticist Henry Goddard might also be a source of Tom's ideas. The work of Goddard and other geneticists was circulated among nativists, and used by the latter to make arguments against the excesses of democracy, which were thought to be manifested in the failure of the melting pot to assimilate new immigrants into American society. In a book widely reprinted around 1920, Goddard studied degeneracy in an American family he called the "Kallikaks." The Kallikaks are "a family of good English blood of the middle class." However, Goddard explains, "a scion of this family, in an unguarded moment, step[ped] aside from the paths of rectitude and with the help of a feeble-minded girl, start[ed] a line of mental defectives that is truly appalling." The "degeneracy" of the Kallikak family is thus "the result of the defective mentality and bad blood," from the feeble-minded prostitute, "having been brought into the normal family of good blood." Goddard concludes by decrying the effects of mixing good and bad genes, reasoning that it can only produce mental and moral defects, such as feeble-mindedness, madness, alcoholism, sexual perversity, and criminality. See Henry Herbert Goddard, *The Kallikak Family: A Study in the Heredity of Feeble-Mindedness* (New York: Macmillan, 1912), 50, 69.

34. The nativist accusation that new immigrants did not earn their wealth according to the virtuous ethics of Protestant work qualifies Michaels's argument that, during the twenties, citizenship was no longer imagined to be "a condition that could be achieved through one's own actions" but, rather, "an identity that could better be understood as inherited" (Michaels, "The Vanishing American," 223).

35. Higham, *Strangers in the Land,* 172.

36. Lothrop Stoddard, *The Rising Tide of Color against White World-Supremacy* (New York: Charles Scribner's Sons, 1920), 288.

37. Higham, *Strangers in the Land,* 265.

38. Michaels, "The Souls of White Folk," 195.

39. Charles W. Gold, *America: A Family Matter* (New York: Charles Scribner's Sons, 1922), 149–50, 165.

40. Stoddard, *The Rising Tide of Color,* 266.

41. Higham, *Strangers in the Land,* 322–23.

42. Sigmund Freud, *The Interpretation of Dreams,* trans. James Strachey (New York: Avon, 1965), 660.

43. My formulation is drawn from Tom Nairn, who persuasively argues that nationalism, like the old Roman god Janus, watches over the passage to modernity. "As human kind is forced through its strait doorway, it must look desperately back into the past, to gather strength wherever it can be found for the ordeal of 'development.'" (Tom Nairn, *The Break-Up of Britain,* rev. ed. [London: Verso, 1981], 348–49).

44. Adams later claimed to have always been aware of the originality of the term "American dream," and to have lobbied his publisher to use the term in the book's title. In a letter composed fifteen years after the initial publication of *The Epic of America,* Adams wrote: "Ellery Sedgwick [editor of the *Atlantic Monthly*] said that I could not call my 'Epic of America,' 'The American Dream' as I wanted to. His objection was that no red-blooded American would pay $3.50 for a dream. Red-blooded Americans have always been willing to gamble their last peso on a dream and the one phrase from my whole book which has become journalese is 'the American

dream'" (letter to Leland Case, 13 May 1946, in Allan Nevins, *James Truslow Adams: Historian of the American Dream* [Urbana: University of Illinois Press, 1968], 296).

45. *Publishers' Weekly* 155 (11 June 1949): 2396. *The Epic of America* was translated into more than a dozen foreign languages and republished in numerous American editions through the 1960s.

46. Fredric Jameson offers this formulation in a different context; see his "Criticism in History," in *The Ideologies of Theory: Essays 1971–1986*, vol. 1, *Situations of Theory* (Minneapolis: University of Minnesota Press, 1988), 125.

47. This helps account for why, at the time of the book's initial printing, an excerpt from *The Epic* appeared in the ecumenical journal *Catholic World* under the title "Our American Dream" (see *Catholic World* [November 1931]: 216–18). Furthermore, the first book to use the term "American dream" in its title was by Raymond C. Knox and called *Religion and the American Dream* (New York: Columbia University Press, 1934). Knox dedicated his book to James Truslow Adams.

48. On communitarian concerns during the Great Depression, see Warren I. Susman, "The Culture of the Thirties," in *Culture as History: The Transformation of American Society in the Twentieth Century* (New York: Pantheon, 1984), 175. On moral economics and American values in the thirties, see Robert S. McElvaine, *The Great Depression: America, 1929–1941* (New York: Times Books, 1984), 196–223.

49. James Truslow Adams, *The Epic of America* (Boston: Little, Brown, 1931), 411. All further references to this work will be included in the text.

50. As Adams's biographer suggests, the author of *The Epic of America* "carried the principles of T[heodore] R[oosevelt]'s New Nationalism and Wilson's New Freedom into the years of Franklin D. Roosevelt's New Deal" (Nevins, *James Truslow Adams*, 90).

51. Although *The Epic of America* is littered with references to the virtues of rugged frontier individualism, Adams's most explicit commentary on frontier self-making can be found in his essay "Rugged Individualism," *New York Times Magazine* (18 March 1934): 1–2, 11.

52. As Kenneth Lynn points out, in *The Robber Barons* Josephson "strikes the most sympathetic cord in his book by his reference to 'the poverty which darkened the lives of all of them, save [J. P.] Morgan'" (Lynn, "Allan Nevins: An Algerine Captive," *Explorations in Entrepreneurial History* 2 [1949–50]: 249).

53. Satirizing the self-made man has found a number of outlets in American literature since Nathanael West's *A Cool Million* (1934). The most outrageous novel in this tradition may be Ishmael Reed's *Free-Lance Pallbearers* (1967).

6. The Ends of Self-Making

1. John G. Cawelti, *Apostles of the Self-Made Man* (Chicago: University of Chicago Press, 1965), 209–18.

2. David Riesman, *The Lonely Crowd: A Study of the Changing American Character* (New Haven: Yale University Press, 1950), 158–61.

3. Robert L. Heilbroner, *The Quest for Wealth: A Study of Acquisitive Man* (New York: Simon and Schuster, 1956), 241.

4. William H. Whyte Jr., *The Organization Man* (New York: Simon and Schuster, 1956), 182.

5. C. Wright Mills, *The Power Elite* (New York: Oxford University Press, 1956), 349.

6. Ibid., 343, 117.

7. *Fortune* (circa 1960), quoted in John Keats, *Howard Hughes* (New York: Random House, 1966), 289.

8. Hughes's 1948 interview with Dwight Whitney is quoted in James R. Phelan, "Howard Hughes: He Battles for His Empire," *Saturday Evening Post* 236 (9 February 1963): 22.

9. This pattern repeated itself for almost half a century, a period in which Hughes maintained sole ownership of his financial empire by establishing himself as the sole shareholder. Furthermore, over the next thirty-three years Hughes employed an outstanding accountant, named Noah Dietrich, to help guide his wholly owned interests in industries as diverse as movie studios and airlines. Later, Dietrich and others would act as public stand-ins for the recluse Hughes.

10. Quoted in Phelan, "Howard Hughes," 18.

11. Quoted in ibid., 19.

12. See Stephen Fay, Lewis Chester, and Magnus Linklater, *Hoax: The Inside Story of the Howard Hughes-Clifford Irving Affair* (New York: Viking, 1972), 32.

13. The story of Rosemont Enterprises, Inc. is expounded in ibid., 154, 202.

14. Quotation from *Newsweek* cited in Albert B. Gerber, *Bashful Billionaire: The Story of Howard Hughes* (New York: Lyle Stuart, 1967), 349.

15. There may have been another motivation as well. Hughes had been losing dominion over his empire since 1970 and, before the end of 1972, the Hughes Tool Company (founded by his father and the flagship of his financial enterprises) was offered to the public under a new name, the Summa Corporation. The fact that all of this was accomplished largely without Hughes's consent suggests the degree to which he had lost control over himself and his corporate empire. These details regarding Hughes's life can be found in Donald L. Barlett and James B. Steele, *Empire: The Life, Legend, and Madness of Howard Hughes* (New York: Norton, 1979).

16. Excerpts from the transcript of the televised telephone interview with Hughes are reproduced in the 10 January 1972 editions of the *New York Times* and the *Los Angeles Times*.

17. Fay et al., *Hoax*, 142.

18. Despite Hughes's apparent bad memory, the panel of journalists unanimously agreed that the disembodied voice sounded authentic. Later, voice-print analysis experts agreed that the voice was, indeed, Howard Hughes's.

19. Fay et al., *Hoax*, 154, 202. As it turned out, the "as told to" autobiography of Howard Hughes was never published. A month after Hughes's 9 January 1972 telecommunicated interview, evidence was uncovered that forced the publishers to openly acknowledge that the book was not authentic but, rather, essentially a product of Clifford Irving's skills as a plagiarist.

20. Lee Iacocca with William Novak, *Iacocca: An Autobiography* (New York: Bantam, 1984), xv. All further references to this work will be included in the text.

21. Iacocca confirms his silence when, in the autobiography, he explains that

only when he is "safely out of camera range" did he allow himself to mutter an expletive (ibid., xiv).

22. Chrysler television commercial, 2 June 1982, quoted in James A. Benson and Judith M. Thorpe, "Chrysler's Success Story: Advertising as Anecdotes," *Journal of Popular Culture* 25 (winter 1991): 129.

23. Only when he was forced to wear "ragged" clothes during the Great Depression does Iacocca directly apply the rags-to-riches formula to himself (8).

24. Amanda Bennett, "President Iacocca?" *Wall Street Journal*, 28 June 1982, 1.

25. Excerpts from Ross Perot's news conference are reproduced in the *New York Times*, 2 October 1992, A20.

26. Although her frame of reference—Frank Capra films—is different from my own, see Linda Schulte-Sasse's "Meet Ross Perot: The Lasting Legacy of Capraesque Populism," *Cultural Critique* 25 (fall 1993): 104–5, for an overlapping analysis of Perot's speech.

27. Susan Powter, *Stop the Insanity!* (New York: Simon and Schuster, 1993), 10. All further references to this work will be included in the text. Powter repeats the mantra "I call myself: a housewife who figured it out" in many forums, including her book *The Pocket Powter* (New York: Simon and Schuster, 1994), 250.

28. Stuart Hirsch, president of A-Vision (the entertainment company that distributes Susan Powter videos) and former chief operating officer of King World (which distributes the *Oprah Winfrey Show*), comments on Powter's celebrity potential with direct reference to Oprah: "I haven't dealt with a star with her potential since Oprah." Hirsch is quoted in Steve McClellan, "Multimedia Taps Powter," *Broadcasting & Cable* 123 (1 November 1993): 24.

29. Harry F. Waters and Patricia King, "Chicago's Grand New Oprah," *Newsweek* 104 (31 December 1984): 51.

30. Although the majority of their viewers are white women, both Oprah and Powter reach diverse audiences. Much has been made, for example, about the discord between Oprah and her black female viewership over her romance with Stedman Graham, a onetime fashion model. Powter's first husband (the "Prince") is Mexican American, which has reportedly helped her generate a sizable following among Latino women.

31. Jean Baudrillard also calls this "the satellitization of the real," which collapses the distinction between the private and the public realm and sends the domestic sphere into orbit. See his essay "The Ecstasy of Communication," trans. John Johnston, in *The Anti-Aesthetic: Essays on Postmodern Culture*, ed. Hal Foster (Port Townsend, Wash.: Bay Press, 1983), 128.

32. Oprah Winfrey, quoted in Robert Waldron, *Oprah!* (New York: St. Martin's Press, 1987), 191.

33. Audience share statistics quoted in Pat Colander, "Oprah Winfrey's Odyssey," *New York Times*, 12 March 1989, sec. 2, 37.

34. Oprah Winfrey, quoted in Barbara Grizzuti Harrison, "The Importance of Being Oprah," *New York Times Magazine*, 11 June 1989: 54, and Marcia Ann Gillespie, "Winfrey Takes All," *Ms.* 17 (November 1988): 50.

35. My explanation of the New Age movement's concept of "prosperity consciousness"—including its indebtedness to the older New Thought movement—is

drawn from J. Gordon Melton, *New Age Almanac* (New York: Visible Ink Press, 1991), 433.

36. "Oprah's Story" is the opening section of Bob Greene and Oprah Winfrey's *Make the Connection: Ten Steps to a Better Body—and a Better Life* (New York: Hyperion, 1996), 13–17. The sketch, which is the only sustained autobiographical statement published by Winfrey to date, basically transcribes *Oprah*'s 22 November 1993 "Weight Loss Show." It is symptomatic of current manuals on success that *Make the Connection* puts New Age self-awareness into the service of changing one's body image.

37. Susan Powter, quoted in Mary McNamara, "She Says," *Ms.* 7 (July–August 1996): 72.

38. Susan Powter, quoted in Alex Witchel, "Susan Powter," *New York Times Magazine* (31 October 1993): 61.

39. Christopher Lasch, *The Culture of Narcissism: American Life in an Age of Diminishing Expectations* (New York: Norton, 1978), 53.

40. A year later, Powter settled with the Frankels by agreeing to pay the latter $2.8 million, mostly in future earnings, in order to sever business ties with the pair.

41. Susan Powter, quoted in Jill Jordan Sieder, "A Painful Business Exercise," *U.S. News & World Report* 120 (18 March 1996): 66–67.

42. Gerald Frankel, quoted in Lisa Faye Kaplan, "Fitness Sage: Take a Powter and Rule the World," *Gannett News Service* (31 January 1995).

43. Susan Powter, quoted in Jeannine Stein, "Powter Keg," *Los Angeles Times,* 14 September 1994, E5.

44. Powter, quoted in Sieder, "A Painful Business Exercise," 67.

45. In fact, Powter anticipates the likelihood that the viewer will misrecognize her "after" portrait in the pages of *Stop the Insanity!*; the caption under the photo reads, in part: "Nobody will believe it's me? Who else could it be? Look at the hair" (280).

Epilogue: The Return of the Self-Made Man

1. Arnold Schwarzenegger with Douglas Kent Hall, *Arnold: The Education of a Bodybuilder* (New York: Simon and Schuster, 1977), 3. All further references to this work will be included in the text.

2. Arnold Schwarzenegger, quoted in George Butler, *Arnold Schwarzenegger: A Portrait* (New York: Simon and Schuster, 1990), 96.

3. J. Hoberman, "Terminal Systems," review of *Terminator 2: Judgment Day, Village Voice* 36 (9 July 1991), 49. For an overview of Arnold Schwarzenegger's movie career prior to the release of *Terminator 2,* see Hoberman's essay "The Self-Made Man," *Village Voice* 36 (12 February 1991), 53ff.

4. Schwarzenegger, quoted in Butler, *Arnold Schwarzenegger,* 99.

5. George Butler, quoted in Molly O'Neill, "The Arm Fetish," *New York Times,* 3 May 1992, sec. 9, 1.

6. Steve Michalik, quoted in Paul Solotaroff, "The Power and the Gory," *Village Voice* 36 (29 October 1991), 33. My discussion of Michalik's self-making and

self-destruction is taken from Solotaroff's engaging account of the bodybuilder's bout with steroids.

7. Ibid., 156.

8. Michalik, quoted in ibid., 30.

9. Ibid., 156.

Index

Abbott, Jacob, xix, 67
Adams, James Truslow, 97–101,
154–55 n. 44, 155 n. 50; *The Epic
of America*, 97–101, 154–55,
n. 44–45, 155 n. 47, 155 n. 51;
"Our American Dream," 155 n. 47;
"Rugged Individualism,"
155 n. 51
advertisements. *See* autobiography
African Americans, xiv, xxii–xxiii, 65,
81–85, 95, 152 n. 13; and black nationalism, xxix, 43, 51–62, 84; and
black womanhood, 42–49, 52, 58,
117; and business enterprise, xv–xvi,
xxvi–xxix, 102, 133, 146 n. 53,
146 n. 6; and the Great Migration,
53; and individualism, xxviii, 35–38,
53–56; and individualism, limits of,
xxviii, 32, 54, 56; middle-class, 43,
47, 144 n. 28; and racial integration
(aka "social equality"), 52, 84;
working-class, 43–44, 47, 58–59,
144 n. 30. *See also* formulas—
class mobility: "rags-to-riches,"
nontraditional appropriation of;
formulas—racial uplift; formulas—
slave narrative; imperialism, and
Africa; lynching; segregation
Aiken, Albert, 10
Alcott, Louisa, 67

Alger, Horatio, Jr., xx, xxvi, 1–3, 5,
10–11, 15–17, 27, 30, 67, 78, 122,
130, 139 n. 1, 143 n. 6; *Mark, the
Matchboy*, 5; *Ragged Dick*, xx–xxi,
1–2, 5, 11, 137 n. 29, 139 n. 13,
143 n. 6; *Tattered Tom*, 15–17, 67.
See also formulas—class mobility:
"luck-and-pluck"
American dream, xii, xv, 79–80,
97–101, 109, 111–12, 114,
151 nn. 2, 4; origins of, xxix, 80, 97,
101, 154–55 n. 44
Anderson, Benedict, 136 n. 25
anticommunism, 13, 98, 101
Antin, Mary, xiv, 64–69, 90, 114,
149 nn. 49–50; and *Atlantic
Monthly*, 149 n. 49; and educational
uplift, 65–66, 68; and Hale House
Natural History Club, 69; and Progressive Era, xx, 62, 65; *The Promised Land*, 64–71, 99, 149 nn. 49,
51; *They Who Knock at Our Gates*,
64; and Transcendentalism, 69, 99.
See also salesmanship
anti-Semitism, 81–82, 89, 91, 110,
112, 153 n. 24. *See also* nativism;
racism; stereotypes
Armstrong, Nancy, 25
Asian Americans. *See* immigrants;
Chinese, Japanese, Korean

161

Jeffrey Louis Decker received a doctorate in American Civilization from Brown University. He was an Andrew W. Mellon Faculty Fellow in the Humanities at Harvard University, and teaches American studies and American literature at the University of California, Los Angeles.